BY THE GRACE OF G-D

LEARNING ON THE JOB

JEWISH CAREER LESSONS

Adapted freely from the teachings of

The Rebbe
Rabbi Menachem Mendel Schneerson
of righteous memory

Compiled and adapted by
Dovid Zaklikowski

Art by
Yitzchok Moully

HASIDIC
archives

Learning on the Job © 2016 Hasidic Archives
www.HasidicArchives.com
HasidicArchives@gmail.com
Facebook.com/HasidicArchives

· ·

All rights reserved, including the right to
reproduce this book or portions thereof,
in any form, without prior permission,
in writing, from Hasidic Archives

· ·

ISBN 978-1-944875-00-8
Design by Design is Yummy and
Hasidic Archives Studios
Illustrations by Design Is Yummy
Printed in Singapore

Dedicated to
Rabbi Simcha Zirkind
who lovingly dedicated his life,
as a Chabad representative,
to the Jewish communities in
Tunisia, Canada, and beyond.

The Rebbe,
Rabbi Menachem Mendel Schneerson

CONTENTS

In the beginning...	15	
Accountant	16	
Archivist	17	
Employment as Assistance	18	
Astronomer	20	
Astronomer II	21	
Architect	22	
Artist	24	
Artist II	25	
Making Art Affordable	26	
Artist III	28	
Astronaut	29	
Attorney General	30	
Banker	32	
Bookkeeper	33	

Imprisoned by Wealth	34
Broadcaster	36
Broadcaster II	38
Bus Driver	39
Butcher	40
A Businessman Spreads Light	42
Cardiologist	44
Cardiologist II	45
Chemist	46
Coast Guard	48
Computer Programmer	49
Like a Computer	50
Construction Worker	52
Construction Worker II	53
Dietician	54
Electrician	55

Engineer	56
Banking Happiness	58
Entrepreneur	60
Entrepreneur II	61
Entrepreneur III	62
Peace of Mind	64
When to Give Advice	67
Factory Worker	68
Farmer	69
Farmer II	70
Firefighter	71
Firefighter II	72
Exchanging One Business for Another	74
Fisherman	76
Fisherman II	77
Gardener	78

Gardener II	79
Envy the Businessman	**80**
Home Designer	82
Horseman	83
Business, Faith and Charity	**84**
Internship	88
Insurance Broker	89
Jeweler	90
Jeweler II	91
A Positive Influence	**92**
Judge	94
Jumper	95
Jumper II	96
Laundry Person	97
Lawyer	98
Lawyer II	99

Safe Endeavors	**100**
Just Life Grandfather	**103**
Lawyer III	104
Locksmith	105
Locksmith II	106
Manicurist	107
Don't Deny Them a Livelihood!	**108**
Marketer	110
Mechanic	112
Mechanic II	113
What Is Retirement?	**114**
Merchant	116
Microbiologist	117
Mortgage Broker	118
How to Speak to an Employee	**120**
Mountain Climber	122

Mountain Climber II	123
Musician	124
Keeping Business Fresh	**126**
Nurse	128
Optometrist	129
Optometrist II	130
Optometrist III	132
Pharmacist	133
A Model Businessman	**134**
Pharmacist II	136
Physician	137
Physician II	138
Physician III	140
Physician IV	141
A Lesson for the Phlebotomist	**142**
Pilot	144

Pilot II	145	Senator	159	**Inside Information**	176
Pilot III	146	Ship Captain	160	Teacher	178
President	147	**Another's**		Telegraph Messenger	179
Prison Warden	148	**Livelihood**	162	Telemarketer	180
Lecture with a		Shoemaker	164	Train Conductor	181
Secret Agenda	150	Shoemaker II	165	Vintner	182
Rancher	152	Slaughterer	166	Watchmaker	183
Sailor	153	**Location Matters**	168	**The Professor's**	
Sailor II	154	Soldier	170	**Journal**	184
Secretary	155	Soldier II	171	Afterword: An	
Not Just a		Surgeon	172	**Uplifting Outlook**	186
Business Trip	156	Tailor	174	**Credits & Sources**	190
Passive Investors	157	Taxi driver	175	**Acknowledgements**	194
Security Guard	158				

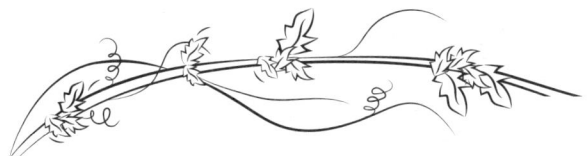

Who is wise? The one who learns from everyone.

– Ethics of Our Fathers 4:1

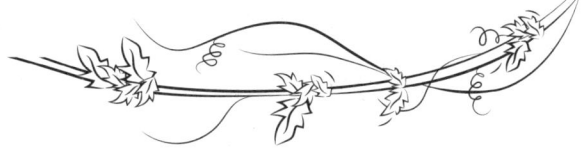

Everything you hear or see has a lesson for you in your service of G-d.

– Rabbi Israel Baal Shem Tov
Founder of the Hasidic movement

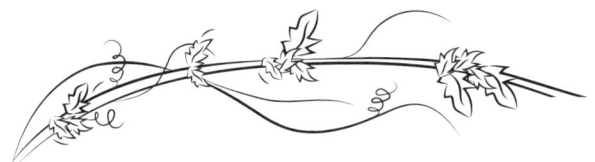

In everything you hear or see, in everything that becomes known to you, there is a message specifically for you. As a person with free will, you may decide how to interpret these messages.

– The Rebbe, Rabbi Menachem Mendel Schneerson

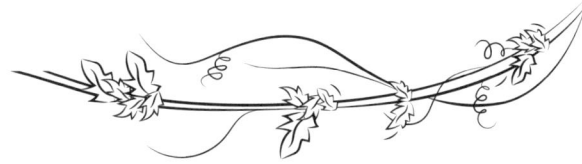

IN THE BEGINNING...

Torah *[toi-ra]: the Bible (Five Books of Moses); teaching; the Torah scroll; used loosely for the general corpus of Jewish teachings.*

In 1313 BCE, the year 2448 from the creation of the world, G-d gave the Torah to the Jewish nation on Mount Sinai, following their exodus from Egypt. The Torah is G-d's wisdom, expressed in human terms. Even the stories in the Torah contain deep lessons for our daily lives. When we study Torah, our finite intellect grasps the infinite. Every generation has its Torah scholars, and their teachings and interpretations are incorporated into the body of rabbinic literature, which is considered part of the Torah itself. Torah is studied by children and adults, lay people and scholars.

Mitzvah(s) *[mits-va]: commandment; precept; connection; used loosely for a good deed.*

The Torah is G-d's wisdom, and the mitzvahs are His will. The Hebrew word mitzvah comes from the root meaning "connection." Each of the Torah's 613 mitzvahs may be envisioned as a single strand in a rope that binds us to our creator. The infinite G-d chose us, finite beings, to be His emissaries in this world, to observe the mitzvahs, giving significance to our observance. This recognition brings us joy and humility.

Hasidism *a movement founded in the 18th century by Rabbi Israel the son of Eliezer, who became known as the Baal Shem Tov. Hasidic philosophy uses the teachings of Kabbalah to examine the deeper significance of Torah and mitzvahs.*

The Baal Shem Tov taught that "G-d wants the service of the heart," that mitzvahs performed with sincere devotion are precious as scholarly accomplishments. He emphasized serving G-d with love and joy, and recognizing the divine individual providence that governs even the smallest details of creation. Chabad Hasidism calls for the intellectual engagement in the service of G-d. The teachings explain how the mind may be used to control the heart, allowing one to subdue her or his negative desires and tendencies and live a life of holiness.

Note: Many of the lessons in this book are presented as metaphors, a technique the Rebbe often employs to make ideas more accessible. These are free adaptations. Any errors are those of the compiler.

ACCOUNTANT

When an accountant prepares taxes, one of the first steps is to calculate the client's income bracket. The more money earned, the higher the bracket and the more taxes will be owed. Sometimes even a small increase in income can push a person into a higher bracket.

If you regularly give a certain sum to charity, and then you add even a small amount of money, you may enter a new "bracket." Only in this system, the higher your bracket, the greater your reward.

ARCHIVIST

The purpose of an archive is to preserve valuable documents and records and to transmit moral lessons from generation to generation.

The Torah is a living archive that preserves and transmits the history and heritage of our people. While it contains many numbers and facts, it also provides a moral compass by which generations of Jews have guided their lives.

EMPLOYMENT AS ASSISTANCE

When David Deitsch asked the Rebbe how he could assist Israel in 1973, he was expecting to be told to make a donation to one of the many Chabad organizations there. To his surprise, the Rebbe told him, "Israel needs industry. There are many immigrants coming to Israel. I suggest you build a plant in Israel."

The owner of the New Haven–based Deitsch Industries began exploring the possibility of an Israeli division. It was clear from the beginning that this would not be a profitable business venture, but rather an investment in the future of Israel.

Mr. Deitsch appointed his son-in-law Meir Zeiler to head the venture. It was difficult going, however. Local bureaucracy put up obstacles, and Mr. Deitsch turned to the Rebbe, telling him that the Israelis seemingly "don't want us, [and] don't need us."

"They need you, and you need them," the Rebbe calmly told him. "A lot of people need you, and they will have great benefit from the factory."

In 1979, after much sweat and millions of dollars, Flocktex Industries opened its doors in Kiryat Malachi, manufacturing upholstery and curtain fabric, most of which it exported. The company employs over 150 workers and has become a model for other factories in the area.

The Rebbe, during a public gathering, in conversation with David Deitsch.

ASTRONOMER

A lunar year has approximately eleven fewer days than a solar year. The Jewish calendar follows the lunar cycle. To keep the Jewish holidays synchronized with the four seasons, an extra month is added to the Hebrew calendar seven times in every nineteen years. The leap year makes up for time lost in the past and compensates for time that will be lost in the future.

You can and should make up for lost opportunities. Even if you think no opportunity has been missed, it's a good idea to guard against possible loses in the future by performing extra good deeds whenever you have the chance.

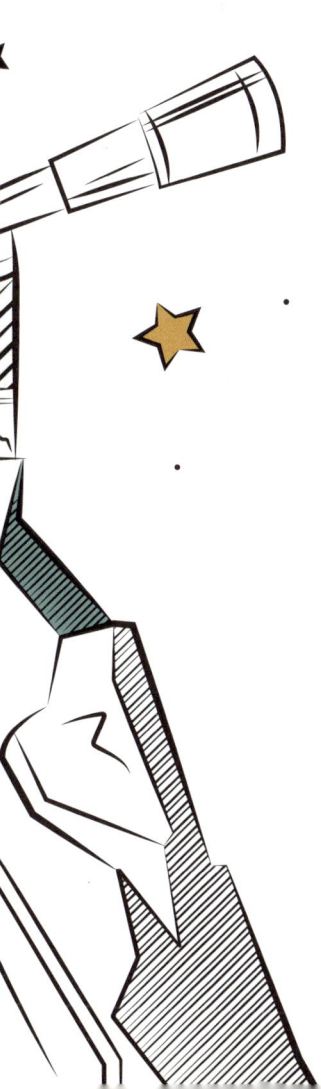

ASTRONOMER II

The moon's monthly cycle of waxing and waning makes it appear larger on some nights and smaller on others. There are even nights when it is completely hidden, yet it always reappears.

Every day will bring challenges, some small and some large. Each challenge we overcome becomes a force for good in the world, a light shining in the darkness.

ARCHITECT

Before you build your dream home, you first decide how to divide the space and choose the materials you want to use. The architect draws up the plans, and only then does the construction crew begin their work.

When G-d created the world, He made the plans first. On the first day He said, "Let there be light." This is the spiritual light that permeates the world. G-d's plan, the ultimate purpose of creation, is that we reveal this light by overcoming challenges and performing good deeds. G-d "built" the entire physical world—heavens and earth, minerals, vegetation, animals and humans—for the fulfillment of this plan.

On a personal level, when you wake up in the morning with renewed strength, the first thing you should do is make a plan. Plan to reveal the spiritual light in everything around you. In the course of your day, if you find yourself unsure how to proceed, consult the plan for guidance.

ARTIST

The artist uses lifeless objects—brushes, paint and canvas—to create a lively painting.

Our art is to use physical objects in the service of G-d, elevating them to a lively spiritual plane.

ARTIST II

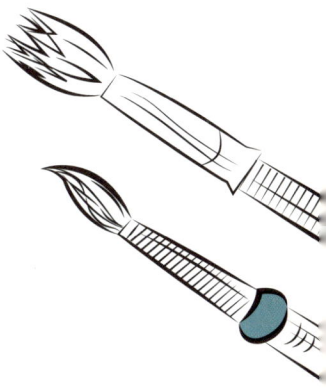

The talented artist portrays not only a scene or a person, but also internal emotions and spirit.

Nothing happens by chance. Wherever you are, G-d placed you there to reveal the G-dly spark, the spirit in everything around you.

MAKING ART AFFORDABLE

Baruch Nachshon arrived in the United States from Israel in 1963 to pursue his education in art. At the age of 19, during a difficult period, he had become attracted to the teachings of Hasidism and started a correspondence with the Rebbe. Now the 24-year-old artist and his wife came to meet the Rebbe for the first time.

In that meeting, the Rebbe guided Mr. Nachshon to work on creating "kosher art." When he agreed, the Rebbe offered to fund his studies at the School of Visual Arts in New York City. The Rebbe also paid for the young couple's monthly rent and other expenses.

Mr. Nachshon went on to create a unique genre, depicting mystical concepts and fantastical scenery. "I don't copy the styles of the world," the artist says. "For me, all the inspiration comes from the point of inspiration—heaven."

Back in Israel after graduating from art school, Mr. Nachshon led a secluded life, rarely venturing out of his studio and study. His financial situation began to deteriorate.

After a 1977 exhibit in London, the artist travelled to New York and met with the Rebbe again. He asked if the Rebbe would like to see some of his art. Wanting to encourage people to purchase the art, the Rebbe offered to make an exhibit in one of the wings at Lubavitch world headquarters.

The Rebbe was the first to visit the exhibit. Studying each piece, the Rebbe offered a suggestion: "You depict the soul of Judaism well. However, Judaism is also about the body. The body is central to Jewish observance. In the future, try to express the actions of our forefathers—Jewish observance—so that the general

Artist Baruch Nachshon at work in his studio.

public will have an understanding and feel a connection to the art."

After the exhibit, the Rebbe called Mr. Nachshon into his private study and asked if there had been any sales. Very few, the artist said. "When the people heard the price of the art, they fainted."

The Rebbe smiled at this and told Mr. Nachshon to sell to healthy people. In addition, he advised him to make an effort to print lithographs, so that his art would be affordable for every family.

Over the years, the Rebbe advised the editors of various magazines to employ Mr. Nachshon to create their cover art.

ARTIST III

A shadow could be seen as something negative, a dark blot on a beautiful scene. To the artist, however, a shadow is a useful tool, emphasizing details and adding brightness to other parts of a picture.

When you feel that your day has been darkened by a shadow, try to look at things from the artist's perspective: see the darkness as an opportunity to add more beauty and brightness to the world.

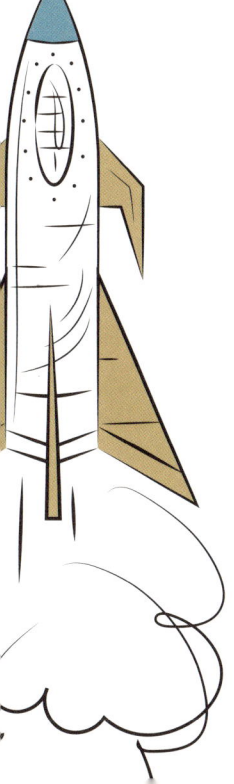

ASTRONAUT

An astronaut in space follows specific rules about how to eat, dress, and even sleep. A slight deviation could cause the loss of billions of dollars and endanger the other astronauts in the spaceship.

Your service of G-d, even the smallest detail, affects you and your family, your surroundings, and ultimately the entire world.

ATTORNEY GENERAL

The attorney general prosecutes crimes, but also educates the citizenry in order to create a safer community.

Don't just tell your community members, friends and family what they are doing wrong. Educate and inspire them to do what's right.

BANKER

When you deposit money in the bank, you know that while you do not have it in your hand, it's there for safekeeping and still belongs to you.

Every good deed brings a reward. You may not see it immediately, but know that it is in the "bank," and one day it will be "cash in your pocket."

BOOKKEEPER

A bookkeeper ensures that the books are balanced—that debits and credits are in equilibrium. If there is a discrepancy, be it one dollar or a thousand, something is amiss.

Our spiritual books, too, need to be balanced. We may consider one mitzvah or good deed to be worth more than another, but if any opportunity is neglected, the books will not be balanced.

IMPRISONED BY WEALTH

Howard Hughes was, among other things, a film producer, real estate mogul, business tycoon, aviator and aerospace engineer. He was one of the richest individuals in the world when he became an obsessive recluse.

He held business meetings in secret locations, and built a security system to protect his holdings and companies that, according to his biographer, was "more encompassing than that used by the [United States] Defense Department."

The billionaire also sought to control the behavior of his employees: "Do not fraternize with persons outside the office," he instructed aides. "Do not engage in long, unnecessary conversations with secretaries.... Tell your wife as little as possible."

Losing a large contract for the U.S. government in 1947 intensified his paranoia. Though it did not significantly affect his wealth, the loss made a large dent in his ego and emotional psyche.

He had no friends, only aides. His wife had to make an appointment to see him; he had no children. "Had [he] had a friend in the world in 1958, that person would have encouraged or arranged psychiatric care for him before it was too late," his biographer writes. "But always a loner, Hughes had no true friends and no close family ties, no one to say, 'Howard, you need help.'"

His situation deteriorated slowly. He commanded those around him not to breathe on him, would balk if someone touched him accidentally, and used tissues to protect himself from imagined germs. On the property he rented at a hotel, he designated an entire bungalow for boxes of Kleenex. He cut his nails only once a year, and never cut his hair. His teeth began to decay.

His doctor called Hughes neurotic, but not psychotic. "Howard Hughes may have had some fanciful ideas, but he was not out of touch with reality. He was rational until the day he died," Dr. Wilbur Thain said in a 1979 interview.

On April 5, 1976, Howard Hughes fell unconscious from dehydration in his Mexico hotel and was rushed on a private plane to Houston, Texas. He died en route.

Less than a week later, at a gathering marking his 74th birthday, the Rebbe spoke at length about Hughes and what it means to be free.

"There was an individual who had $2 billion," the Rebbe said. "If he had wanted to, he could have gone anywhere.... However, his life was conducted out of fear of the unknown. All he worried about was who was looking at him, who wanted his money and secrets."

Money did not give him freedom. He couldn't eat what he wanted to, or go where he wanted to. He couldn't do what his heart desired. "It could have been a psychological issue," the Rebbe said, "or a real physical danger to his life. Whatever it was, the fact is that he was imprisoned because of his financial success."

Freedom comes from within, the Rebbe explained. "It is how you feel and how you act. When you are controlled by your money, by your circumstances, by your desires... that is the opposite of freedom. Freedom is doing what is right, what G-d wants you to do."

BROADCASTER

If you don't like what you hear on the radio, it is easy to turn it off or switch to another station.

If the path you are following through life is improper, or if you realize another would be more beneficial, exercise your free will and make a change.

BROADCASTER II

The voice of a broadcaster speaking in one place can be heard all the way around the world.

A mitzvah performed in your home has a spiritual effect on the entire globe.

BUS DRIVER

A single bus route may connect diverse communities to each other: poor and wealthy, new immigrants and citizens.

It is essential to create unity and closeness between the various segments in the Jewish community. After all, we are all part of one holy nation.

BUTCHER

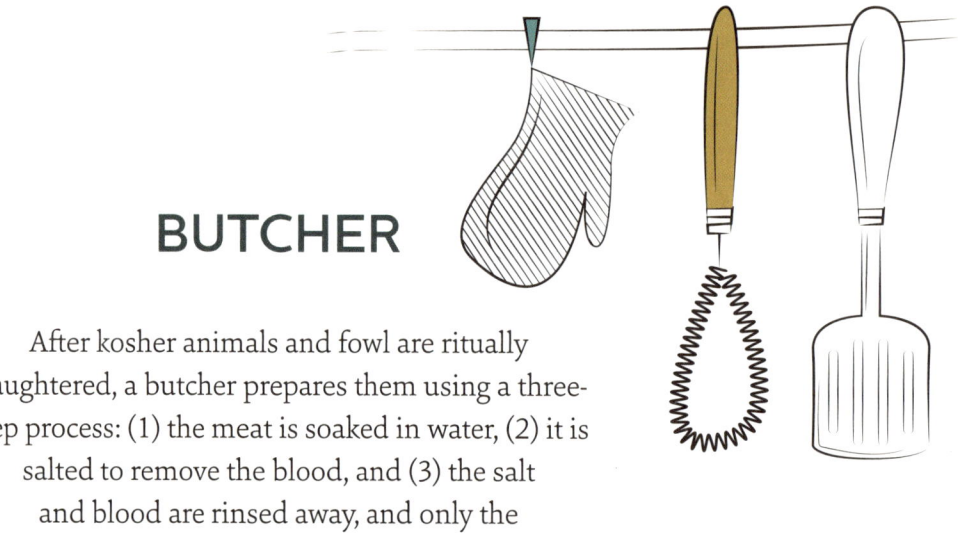

After kosher animals and fowl are ritually slaughtered, a butcher prepares them using a three-step process: (1) the meat is soaked in water, (2) it is salted to remove the blood, and (3) the salt and blood are rinsed away, and only the meat is now visible.

Spiritual endeavors require a similar preparation: (1) soak yourself in prayer and Torah study, (2) remove the "blood" of overindulgence in physical pleasures, and (3) implement what you have studied so that it is apparent in your everyday conduct.

A BUSINESSMAN SPREADS LIGHT

A Holocaust survivor and a proud Jew, David Chase, founder of Chase Enterprises, is one of the richest people in America. Among his holdings are banks, shopping centers, radio stations and real estate.

In 1981, when the Rebbe asked Mr. Chase for a birthday gift, the philanthropist didn't hesitate: he agreed to fulfill the commandment to don tefillin every weekday. He told the Rebbe that he would need three pairs, one for his home in Connecticut, one for his Florida residence and another for his yacht. The Rebbe purchased the three pairs, and Mr. Chase kept his word, wearing the boxes on his head and arm during weekday morning prayers.

Two years later, at a public gathering in honor of the Rebbe's 81st birthday, the Rebbe spoke about Mr. Chase, saying that he was proud of his Jewish identity and observance.

As Mr. Chase sat in the crowd listening, the Rebbe proceeded to relate a story that had happened the year before. Rabbi Moshe Herson, dean of the Rabbinical College of America, sat next to Mr. Chase. It was he who had relayed the story to the Rebbe.

The Rebbe related how Mr. Chase had asked the captain of his yacht which way was east. The following day he asked again. Baffled by the daily request, the captain wondered aloud why the millionaire would need to know.

"I am a religious Jew," Mr. Chase said to the captain. "During our daily prayer service... we pray towards Jerusalem."

The captain was moved by Mr. Chase's commitment to prayer, the Rebbe said. He

The Rebbe in conversation with David Chase.

felt that if a successful businessman takes the time daily to pray properly to G-d, asking for the correct direction, he should think about G-d as well.

Eleven days later, the Rebbe returned to the story. He said that he had since inquired more about the story, and had learned that this encounter had a lasting impact on the captain.

The captain had told Mr. Chase that now, whenever he met family and friends, he talked to them about the importance of thinking about and praying to the Creator of the world. "If all of humanity would think about G-d," the captain had said, "how He is a part of our daily life, the world would not look like such a jungle."

It is our duty to learn, not only from our own experiences, but also from the experiences of others, the Rebbe said. The lesson is that every person can and needs to inspire others, including non-Jews, to be better people. "If you could influence one person to observe the seven universal Noahide laws, just like the captain, who knows how many other people he or she can influence in turn?"

CARDIOLOGIST

If the heart and brain decided to exchange functions, the effect would be disastrous. Extra blood in the brain damages the delicate tissues, and insufficient blood supply to the heart can be fatal. Every organ is perfectly designed to carry out its particular function.

G-d gave each nation a job in this world. The Jews' purpose is to observe the Torah, and the other nations have their own spiritual purposes to fulfill. All the "organs" in this body need each other, but trying to exchange their functions will produce negative results.

CARDIOLOGIST II

The heart and brain perform very different functions in the body, yet the blood vessels and nervous system form connections between them, allowing them to work in tandem. Any disconnection can be fatal.

In the spiritual plane, the heart symbolizes your emotions, the brain your intellect. Both these "organs" are essential to divine service, yet neither can function on its own. Jewish observance requires that our actions be infused with the lifeblood of emotion and intelligence.

CHEMIST

A tiny atom can have a powerful negative effect on much larger matter, as an atom bomb vividly demonstrates.

Conversely, small actions performed by an individual can have a great positive impact on the larger society.

COAST GUARD

The coast guard's job is to keep others safe on the water, but they also have to ensure their own safety.

As we travel the stormy waters of this world, we commit to guard others from harm and rescue those in distress. But it is also our duty to keep ourselves safe by not neglecting our daily spiritual obligations.

COMPUTER PROGRAMMER

A computer can make complex calculations instantaneously. Performing the same calculations by hand would be laborious and time-consuming, and though it may enhance our understanding of the final answer, we may also err in the calculation.

Each mitzvah is the product of a complex spiritual calculation. Even if we don't understand every detail, we can rely on the wisdom of the Torah and the sages. Once we have put the "final answer" into practice, there will be plenty of time for extra study.

LIKE A COMPUTER

Frank Lautenberg was the CEO of Automatic Data Processing, a payroll service company that later became one of the largest computing service companies in the world, when he was appointed chairman of the United Jewish Appeal in 1975.

Shortly after his appointment, Mr. Lautenberg met with the Rebbe to discuss his new role. The UJA was then the most prominent Jewish organization in the United States, raising significant amounts of money for a broad range of social programs.

"I wanted to hear what the Rebbe, whose influence extended across the globe, had to say," Mr. Lautenberg recalled. "I wanted to try and understand what it was that attracted millions of people to him, and I wanted to better understand the responsibilities of a Jewish leader."

The Rebbe encouraged him to think outside the box. "I believe that you are certainly not afraid to do something new... something that can be perceived as a radical change," he said. The Rebbe thought the UJA could be more effective than it was. He recognized the need for fundraising, but said it should not be the organization's only goal. He emphasized the urgent need to combat assimilation, "to prevent the Jewish people from disappearing." The Rebbe also wanted the UJA to allocate more funds to Jewish education.

When Mr. Lautenberg said he would bring up the ideas with the other board members, the Rebbe alluded to Mr. Lautenberg's day job: "The innovation of computers is that what once took two months, two weeks or two hours is now done immediately. This is the reason

Frank Lautenberg

people spend millions on computers.

"You tell me that you will attain results in another two months, two weeks…. That's not the way they work in the computer business!"

If you had an urgent order for computers, the Rebbe asked, "would you sell the computers, or would you start a discussion [with the board]?"

CONSTRUCTION WORKER

Before a construction crew can begin to build a house, they break the ground and dig deep beneath the surface to lay the foundation. The stronger the foundation, the greater the house can become.

To reach your fullest potential, you need to "break ground." Reach beneath your negative habits and natural tendencies to your soul, and allow its light to permeate your being. This will create a strong foundation for a great and holy life.

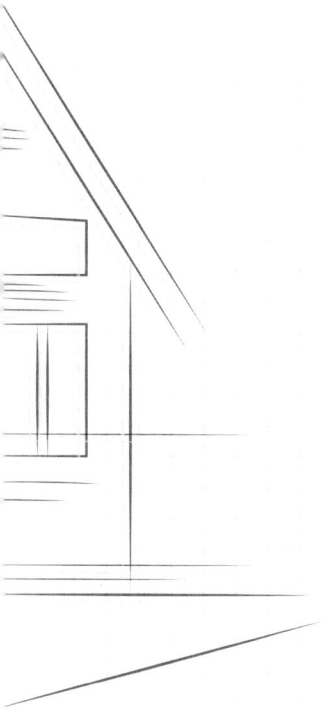

CONSTRUCTION WORKER II

The most vital part of a building is its foundation. To ensure that it resists the elements and erosion, the materials used for the foundation should be of the most durable.

A child needs a strong foundation upon which to build his or her life. A good Jewish education provides an unshakeable foundation that will last into adulthood and beyond, supporting even future generations.

DIETICIAN

Your body requires food to survive. No amount of studying, contemplating and discussing the digestive process will nourish your body. Using the strength gained from food you have eaten, however, you can delve into the details of nutrition, and doing so will bring greater depth and appreciation to your meals.

When you are on a journey towards a Jewish life, begin by doing the mitzvahs. Once your soul has been nourished, then you can deepen your appreciation through study and discussion.

ELECTRICIAN

A light bulb may be screwed into a socket, which is connected by wires and cables to a powerhouse, but it will not light up until the switch is turned on, permitting the current to flow.

Every person possesses a "powerhouse," a soul that is an actual part of G-d. The "switch," however, may be off, preventing the current from flowing as it should. When reaching out to others, all you need to find is the other's "switch"—the correct approach and words—to allow the soul to illuminate his or her life.

ENGINEER

The engineer creates a machine composed of many moving pieces. The consumer uses the machine, but cannot understand all its inner workings. Only the engineer knows the role each tiny piece plays in allowing the machine to function.

In the Torah, G-d has given us a finished product, a comprehensive guide by which to live our lives. While some parts may seem more important or less important to us, only the Engineer knows why each detail is included and its importance to the functioning of the whole.

BANKING HAPPINESS

Banker Edmundo Safdie was all excited. He had come to visit the Rebbe, with the directors of many of his banks, to request blessings for the opening of new branches. He spoke to the Rebbe in French and English.

"We are partners in everything we do all over the world," Mr. Safdie said, referring to his support for Chabad institutions in countries where he did business. "We are always good partners."

A warm man with a jubilant twinkle in his eyes, Mr. Safdie was originally from Syria. He moved from there to Brazil, where he founded Banco Cidade in 1965. In the 1980s he purchased Commerzialbank AG in Geneva, Switzerland, and rebranded it Multi Commercial Bank.

At that meeting in October 1991, he told the Rebbe about a new bank he was planning to open in New York. The Rebbe gave him a blessing: "May G-d Almighty bless you to go from strength to strength, not only in matters of Judaism, but also in your financial endeavors."

Mr. Safdie then introduced the director of the Multi Commercial branch in Geneva. Someone informed the Rebbe that the man was interested in getting married. The Rebbe gave him a blessing for success and said, "It is good for the bank when customers see that the bank's director has a happy family life."

Banker Edmundo Safdie (left) with a business acquaintance.

ENTREPRENEUR

There is a world of difference between a clerk, or any other employee, and the owner of a business. If the business gets into trouble, the clerk may invest much ingenuity, thought and energy into helping it recover. But when the business day ends, the employee goes home and all is forgotten. The business owner, on the other hand, cannot leave his or her troubles at the office.

We all have a personal stake in the future of the Jewish people. If our first efforts to fight assimilation have been unsuccessful, we cannot say, "I did my best, and now I leave it up to G-d." It is necessary to continue to grapple with the problem until it is resolved.

ENTREPRENEUR II

Entrepreneurs make time to balance the books, calculating profits and losses. But if they were to do that all day, they would not have time to build their businesses.

You cannot live your life constantly computing spiritual gains and losses. Certain times are appropriate for that: a few moments of reflection each night, a slightly longer assessment once a month, and a thorough review each year before the High Holidays. These are the times to balance your books, assess your progress and see what needs to be rectified.

ENTREPRENEUR III

If a businessman knows that by earning a penny now he will ultimately lose a million dollars, it is obvious what decision he will make.

A young couple embarking upon married life is undertaking an enormous investment. At this sensitive time, if the families of the bride and groom try to "earn a penny" by arguing over minor details, they may create negative feelings between the couple that will later result in "the loss of millions."

PEACE OF MIND

In the late 1980s, Eduardo Elsztain, chairman of the large Argentinian investment company IRSA, found himself standing on a long line outside Lubavitch world headquarters. It was Sunday, and the Rebbe was distributing crisp dollar bills (to give to charity) and blessings to those who waited.

"I don't understand why I am here," Mr. Elsztain thought to himself. "It costs me 15 dollars to come by taxi from Manhattan and 15 dollars to go back. All this for just one dollar?"

Standing beside him was Rabbi Tzvi Grunblatt, the Chabad representative to Buenos Aires. Mr. Elsztain knew he had to meet the Rebbe, if only for his rabbi's sake.

He had first heard of the Rebbe in 1984, when he traveled to the Soviet Union on a business trip. Rabbi Grunblatt had urged him to use the opportunity to smuggle in Jewish supplies as part of the Rebbe's clandestine efforts to support Jewish life there.

Mr. Elsztain had agreed. He was given Passover provisions to be delivered to a location far from Moscow, and specific directions on how to get there without being detected: He should call a certain number from a public telephone and say that he brought "regards from Grandpa." Then he was to walk, not take a taxi, to a certain crossroads where he would be picked up.

Everything went smoothly, and he found himself in the home of a family with young children. He was moved to think how the Rebbe, far away in New York, was concerned with supplying the needs of this family—this same reflection inspired the family themselves.

The Rebbe in conversation with a couple.

Back in New York, Mr. Elsztain's first meeting with the Rebbe was brief. The Rebbe gave him a dollar, and then another one to give to another person to give to charity.

"When I left, I thought to myself, what happened in these twenty seconds?" Mr. Elsztain said. "I did not look like one of the Rebbe's followers. He did not know me. Yet he gave me a mission to assist someone else whom he does not know [by giving the dollar to charity], and to get another individual that he does not know to do a good deed."

In 1990, Mr. Elsztain was in Brooklyn studying Judaism in the mornings and traveling into Manhattan in the afternoons to find investors for his company. Billionaire George Soros recognized his genius, and gave him $10 million to invest in the Argentinian stock market.

Then, in March 1991, Mr. Elsztain found himself in front of the Rebbe for another short meeting. Soros and others had just given him another $15 million to invest, and he was asking the Rebbe if he should invest it in the stock market.

"I am not so happy about investing money in the stock market," the Rebbe told him. "The stock market does not leave a person with peace of mind.... It disturbs you from sleeping properly."

The Rebbe advised him to transfer the money slowly out of stocks into other investments. "It is not safe. It is better if you invest in something that is safe," the Rebbe said. "Investing in another venture will be good for you."

From then on, IRSA began to focus all of its investments on real estate and agriculture.

Mr. Eduardo Elsztain.

WHEN TO GIVE ADVICE

Diamond dealer Binyomin Wulliger was active in Hasidic circles for many years, serving as a liaison between the Chabad and Sanz communities.

Once he visited the Rebbe after a prolonged absence. "There's something I've wanted to speak to you about for a long time," the Rebbe told him.

When Mr. Wulliger wondered why the Rebbe had not summoned him, the Rebbe explained: "If one wants to give money, it can be given anytime. But if one wants to give advice, regardless of how brilliant and apt it may be, if the person does not approach him or herself, one cannot offer the advice."

The Rebbe proceeded to give his advice to Mr. Wulliger.

FACTORY WORKER

When you walk into a large factory and see many complex machines working on their own, you never doubt that someone built them and continues to maintain them.

Looking at our world with its diverse ecosystems harboring millions of living creatures, can you doubt that Someone created all this and continuously maintains it?

FARMER

One farmer plants a field of wheat, another an orchard of fruit trees. The farmer who planted the wheat will harvest the crop at the end of the growing season, while the farmer who planted the trees must wait many years to enjoy the fruits. Yet the sensual pleasure brought by the fruit far surpasses that brought by the wheat.

At times we may become discouraged if our spiritual toil does not produce immediate results. But remember that a longer process involving greater effort will ultimately yield a sweeter reward.

FARMER II

A farmer who plants trees takes special care of the saplings to ensure that they grow correctly and are not damaged during this vulnerable period. Even the slightest injury in the early stages can have long-term effects on a mature tree.

Similarly, a child's Jewish education requires special care and attention, lest some lasting damage be done. It is up to us to ensure that our children grow straight and strong, and mature into beautiful fruit-bearing "trees."

FIREFIGHTER

When a home is on fire, the firefighters will work diligently to extinguish the flames. If someone is inside, they will not stop to consider the danger, but will immediately jump in and attempt a rescue.

The Jewish world today is in peril. Those who make calculations and do studies about the impact of assimilation may forget the goal: to save our fellow Jews. We are obliged to jump into the fire and do everything we can to reach those in danger.

FIREFIGHTER II

Wood that contains moisture will burn noisily, with much flaring, crackling and popping. The wick on a candle or a gas flame, on the other hand, will burn silently while creating a steady amount of heat and light.

Good deeds bring light and warmth to the world, but they need not be done with fanfare and noise. Do good unabashedly, but in a quiet, refined manner.

EXCHANGING ONE BUSINESS FOR ANOTHER

In the 1980s, Cesar Ades was running a black-market money exchange in Brazil, allowing foreign tourists and businessmen to obtain reais, the Brazilian currency, at a lower rate.

It was a booming business, but it had its downside. Mr. Ades had to contend with rampant crime, shady characters, and the personal danger of being kidnapped. In addition, running an underground "bank" placed him at odds with the Brazilian government.

A quiet, intelligent and generous man, Mr. Ades was also president of the Chabad congregation in Morumbi, S. Paulo. In October 1989, he and his wife traveled to New York with hundreds of other philanthropists for a private audience with the Rebbe at Lubavitch world headquarters.

"I am already involved in the illegal exchange market in Brazil," Mr. Ades told the Rebbe.

The Rebbe was quick to respond: "If something must be done illegally, it is not worthwhile to be involved…"

If stopping abruptly would cause him a substantial loss, the Rebbe said, then he should pull out gradually until all of his business dealings were legal.

Mr. Ades then told the Rebbe that he was considering opening a bank with several partners that would deal with currency exchange and gold.

"If it's done legally, then it is a good idea," the Rebbe said.

The businessman went on to found Banco Rendimento. Today, with 15,000 locations, it is one of Brazil's leading banks and foreign exchange companies.

The Rebbe distributes coins for children to give to charity.

FISHERMAN

A fish needs to be immersed in its element to survive. While it may live for a short time out of the water, in most cases the consequences are immediate.

Jews thrive in the spiritual "water" of mitzvahs. If we leave our element, G-d is kind and allows us the opportunity to return. Over time, however, we may lose our Jewish appearance.

FISHERMAN II

The fish don't say, "Look at the animals on dry land living happy and peaceful lives. Let us go and live with them!"

G-d gave the Jewish nation a unique mission and set of abilities. If we seek to imitate others, we become like fish on dry land.

GARDENER

A tree is dependent on its roots to bring it nourishment from the soil and to anchor it in place. A gardener knows that though the roots are hidden modestly in the ground, they sustain and support the majestic tree, and they require proper care.

Your roots are the patriarchs and matriarchs of the Jewish nation: Abraham, Isaac, Jacob, Sarah, Rebecca, Rachel and Leah. Appreciate your roots and tend them carefully—teach your children about them. In difficult times, take heart in the knowledge that your roots are deep and eternal.

GARDENER II

To one who regularly plants trees and flowers, the process seems natural. Only when one contemplates the variables that come together to produce a good garden—fertile soil, ample rain and sunshine—does one begin to see G-d's hand at work.

Our daily lives seem to be part of the natural order. But when we take the time to contemplate the variables that compose them—a healthy body, sufficient livelihood, loved ones—we cannot help feeling G-d's presence.

ENVY THE BUSINESSMAN

Let me you tell you a story, the Rebbe wrote in a 1967 letter to NASA scientist Dr. Velvl Greene.

Rabbi Shmuel of Lubavitch, the fourth Chabad rebbe, once said to his follower Elia Abeler, "I envy you. You travel and go to markets and fairs, which gives you the opportunity to exchange a Jewish word with a colleague and inspire him to study Talmudic and Hasidic teachings. This creates joy in heaven, and G-d repays the commission in children, life and sustenance. The busier the market and the greater the effort, the greater the livelihood you merit."

Scores of years later, Mr. Abeler related this story to Rabbi Yosef Yitzchak, the sixth Chabad rebbe and Rabbi Shmuel's grandson. Mr. Abeler was set aglow and aflame with those words. His limbs shook as though he had just heard them for the first time that day.

In another letter, in 1986, the Rebbe reiterated this point, adding, "A person should try to arrange his plans in a way that would produce the maximum influence and benefit in one's surroundings, personal benefits and advantages being of secondary consideration. Although in practice, we have seen that success in the area of public good usually brings a greater measure of success in one's personal affairs."

"Every person has places they [alone] can reach," Dr. Greene later said, "and it is your mission to reach out to those to whom no one else has access, and bring them Judaism."

Professor Velvl Greene

HOME DESIGNER

Imagine you were touring a large home in which every room was well appointed and organized. In one room, however, the furniture seemed to be in disarray. Given what you had seen in the rest of the house, you would assume that the interior designer had arranged the room so on purpose, or that it was in the midst of a renovation and would soon be organized.

If some part of the world around you seems to be in disarray, remember that G-d organizes this universe down to the minutest detail. Every part is exactly in accordance with the Designer's specifications.

HORSEMAN

When a horse takes its rider on a journey, it may not know where it is going, and certainly cannot understand the purpose of the journey. It simply looks forward to the food it will receive at the journey's end. Obviously the horse's ignorance does not detract from the importance of the rider's mission.

We travel through this world in physical bodies, dominated by materialistic desires. We may not be able to fathom the existence of a spiritual world or to understand the purpose of our journey. But our inability to grasp these things does not mean they don't exist.

BUSINESS, FAITH AND CHARITY

English businessman Zalmon Jaffe would travel twice a year to spend Jewish holidays with the Rebbe, becoming a familiar and beloved figure at Lubavitch world headquarters. Witty and jovial, Mr. Jaffe attended services and Hasidic gatherings, met with the Rebbe, studied the Rebbe's teachings and reveled in the atmosphere, bringing smiles to all he met.

Mr. Jaffe's correspondence with the Rebbe spans close to 40 years and includes some 260 letters from the Rebbe. The Rebbe guided him in his communal work and offered him business advice. Much of the correspondence, however, is dedicated to the connection between faith, giving charity, and success in business.

When Mr. Jaffe expressed anxiety about his business, the Rebbe urged calm: "Don't worry so much about business. More faith, more livelihood," he wrote. When Mr. Jaffe wrote that "I see that my faith has been justified in the development of the ease of bringing in the imports," the Rebbe responded that he hoped this realization would stimulate "even a greater measure of faith and a corresponding calming effect."

The Rebbe's business advice was often shrewd. He advised Mr. Jaffe to be more adamant with his bank. When he sought a loan, the Rebbe told him, "Request a large one." When the bank was not cooperating and interest rates were too high, the Rebbe told him to look into other banks.

During a particularly rough period, the Rebbe even offered him a loan. "Please let me know if you want it and in what installments you would find it convenient to repay," the Rebbe wrote.

The Rebbe advised Mr. Jaffe to diversify his businesses and investments: "You

The Rebbe in conversation with Mr. Zalmon Jaffe.

should be [doing more] than just rent-collecting."

If the matter was beyond the Rebbe's experience, he did not hesitate to acknowledge it. He advised Mr. Jaffe to speak to an expert on several occasions. Other times the Rebbe made tentative suggestions, admitting that he might be mistaken: "This is outside my competence, and I have made this observation only for what it is worth," he wrote in one letter.

In 1963, the Rebbe wrote that Mr. Jaffe's markup on retail goods seemed too low. If that is the standard markup in the market, or if you are trying to lure new customers, he wrote, then it might be acceptable. "But if both considerations do not apply in this case, a revision of policy is indicated."

In his diaries (published in the series *My Encounter with the Rebbe*), Mr. Jaffe expresses his amazement at the Rebbe's focus on charity. He glowingly describes the Rebbe's distribution of coins to small children to give to charity, and how the Rebbe would stand for hours each Sunday

Zalmon Jaffe, circa 1950's.

distributing dollars for the same purpose.

Traditionally, at least one-tenth of one's income is given to charity. In the Rebbe's first letter to Mr. Jaffe, he wrote that in his opinion Mr. Jaffe should give more than one-tenth. The Rebbe quoted the sages (Talmud, Taanit 9a) that "we can rely on G-d's faithfulness to fulfill His promise of 'to become rich'" when we give extra charity.

Even when business was not good, Mr. Jaffe continued to give regularly. "I was especially pleased to learn from your letter that even when business was not all that could be desired for a while, you maintained your charity at somewhat more than just a tenth," the Rebbe wrote in 1957, "which showed that your faith in G-d did not weaken, and G-d does not remain in debt and rewards generously, so that before long one can see that one's faith was justified."

Later, when Mr. Jaffe reported that business was again doing well, the Rebbe wrote, "I was pleased to read... that you so quickly saw the fulfillment of G-d's promise.... Thus, your pledge... has been returned to you manifold."

Had he pledged more, the Rebbe added, "the benefit would have been so much greater. I trust, however, that this will be a lesson for the future, to remember how trust in G-d is well rewarded."

On another occasion, when profits were growing, the Rebbe told him to increase his donations in kind. "Needless to say, when I write of an increase in charity, I do not mean at the expense of the charity you have been giving all the time, but an increase in the charity you give, which is indicated by the growth of the business, as mentioned above," the Rebbe wrote in 1963.

By giving generously even when business was bad, the Rebbe once wrote, you "confidently and completely realize that G-d is your partner in the business.... The more charity you give, the larger is G-d's share of the partnership."

INTERNSHIP

Interns are never given important roles in a company. Rather, they are given small jobs that allow them to slowly gain experience and expertise. Some interns might feel frustrated at being on the sidelines, but most recognize that the process will eventually lead to better employment.

You may feel frustrated that you are not using your talents to the fullest. You may say to yourself, "I could be a great leader, and yet I am only managing a few workers in a store." Remember that G-d is in charge, and you are in this position for an important reason. Do not despair. Continue on, and always look for ways to use your talents to help the greater community.

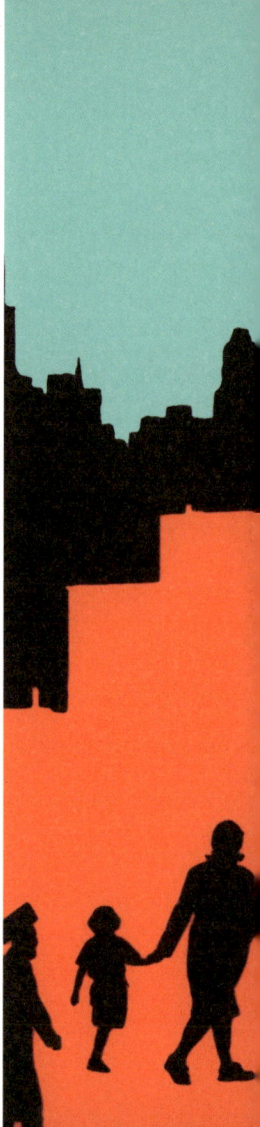

INSURANCE BROKER

Health insurance companies use the money they receive in premiums from healthy members to pay for the care of those who are sick. The healthy members understand that by paying their premiums, they are creating a safety net that will be there if they need it.

We are all members of the greater Jewish community. It is our responsibility to create a safety net that those in need can rely on.

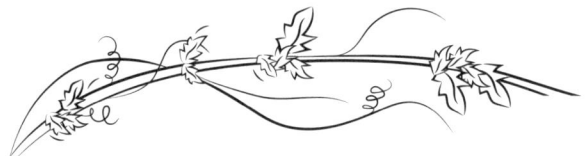

JEWELER

Someone carrying a large package of diamonds and precious metals surely will not complain about its weight.

When you are doing good in a community and you feel that you are becoming overburdened, remember that every person you help is a diamond. You would never put down a load of diamonds because you were tired.

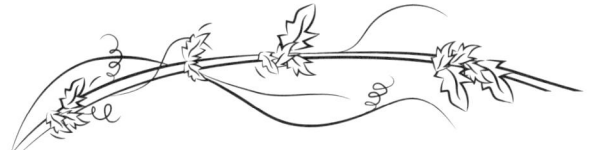

JEWELER II

In order to make a necklace, a jeweler pierces each pearl to create a hole through which a thread can pass.

Every good deed you do is a gem. But at the center of each there needs to be a tiny empty space, an understanding of your own smallness in G-d's presence, and a humble gratitude that He nevertheless asks you to fulfill His will. When they are formed correctly, these jewels, even the smallest ones, will be connected by a common thread: the revelation of G-dliness in the world.

A POSITIVE INFLUENCE

When London diamond dealer Freddy Hager entered the Rebbe's Brooklyn study in the wee hours of the morning, he was feeling down. Mr. Hager had taken over the family business in 1974 on his father's sudden passing.

It was now the summer of 1979, and the diamond business was going through a rough period. After hearing about these difficulties, the Rebbe said with a twinkle in his eye, "You are being too negative, too pessimistic. You need to meet positive people in the diamond trade."

It was a variation on the Hasidic axiom that the Rebbe had frequently mentioned to Mr. Hager: "Think good and it will be good." If he could not do it on his own, the Rebbe suggested, he should befriend positive people and they would help him.

The Rebbe advised him to visit the New York diamond district while he was in town. Mr. Hager said that would be impossible, as he would be flying out shortly to attend a meeting in London.

"Are you sure?" the Rebbe asked. Mr. Hager said he was. The Rebbe shrugged and said, "You should have much success. Have a safe trip, and do not forget to make it your goal to meet positive individuals."

Mr. Hager arrived in London to find that the meeting had been canceled.

A week later, there was a commotion at the London Diamond Bourse. The newly elected president of the New York Diamond Dealers Club, Mr. William Goldberg, had come to visit.

Mr. Goldberg, a large man with a glowing bald spot and flowing gray hair that reached his shoulders, had a boisterous sense of humor and a booming voice. He also had an infectious positive attitude.

William Goldberg

He was known to purchase the most expensive and glamorous diamonds, and that day Mr. Hager arranged a deal for him for one of the finest diamonds available at the time.

Impressed with Mr. Hager, Mr. Goldberg gave him a commission and then handed him his business card and told him to be in touch.

In contrast to the atmosphere of discretion and covert competition that prevailed in the diamond trade, Mr. Goldberg was always happy to see others succeed, and glad to assist whenever he could.

This attitude greatly influenced Mr. Hager. Mr. Goldberg became his mentor, and from then on the two men spoke to each other several times a day.

JUDGE

A judge does research, reviews the law, and looks at what others ruled in the past before issuing a ruling. Afterward, the police make sure that the judgment is enforced.

First do research: learn the Torah laws that apply to your life and how they have been interpreted by the sages. Once you have the final ruling, police yourself so that it is properly carried out.

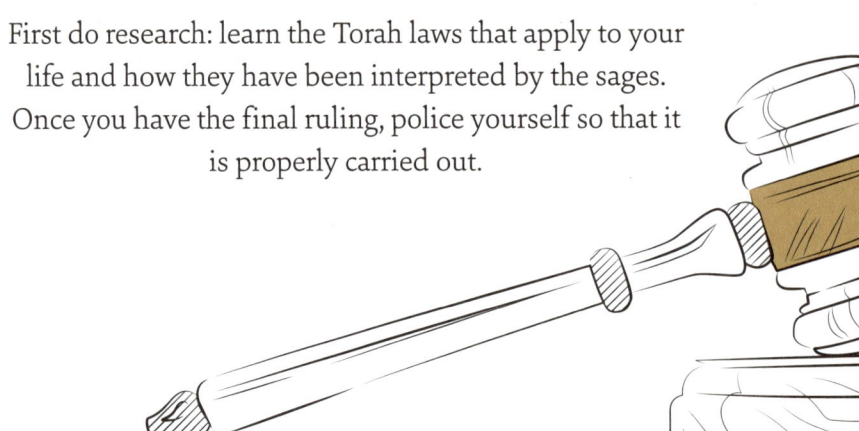

JUMPER

To clear a high obstacle, a jumper first takes several steps backward.

There are many obstacles on the road of life, and we may sometimes need to take a step back and rest before confronting a particular challenge. Be assured that these reversals and periods of calm are only for the purpose of reaching greater heights.

JUMPER II

Jumpers need a running start to clear an obstacle. The further away they begin from their target, the more momentum they have.

If you have inadvertently taken a few steps backward on the path of Jewish life, use this distance to give yourself a "running start." You may reach even greater spiritual heights than before.

LAUNDRY PERSON

If you were to soil your shirt, you would not throw it out. Dirty laundry simply needs washing and ironing to be clean and good as new.

If your soul has become soiled during its sojourn in this physical world, do not give up hope. Immerse yourself in daily prayers and Torah study, and your soul will soon begin to shine with renewed light.

LAWYER

Defense lawyers approach their clients with empathy. Only by trying to understand their clients' motivations can the lawyers hope to defend them successfully.

Consider yourself a defense lawyer for your fellows. If you see people involved in questionable activities, approach them with empathy, try to understand their motivations, and judge them favorably.

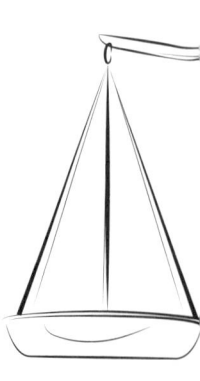

LAWYER II

Lawyers who break the law are disbarred and their opinions are disregarded.

When a person's actions are not in sync with Torah values, it will certainly have an effect on his or her opinions.

SAFE ENDEAVORS

In 1974, Nicaragua, under the dictatorship of Anastasio Somoza Debayle, was trying to recover from a devastating earthquake. Sensing a business opportunity, Massachusetts lawyer Jeffrey Kimball approached Nicaragua's ambassador to the United States, Guillermo Sevilla Sacasa (Debayle's brother-in-law), offering the country his assistance.

Mr. Kimball had come up with a plan to build affordable housing quickly. The ambassador liked it and had it approved. Only one obstacle remained: the project required a $5 million loan.

A bank approved the loan, with one condition. Mr. Kimball himself would need to sign off—the bank wanted the lawyer's personal property as collateral.

Mr. Kimball hesitated. He didn't want to put his own finances on the line, but he felt the deal was too good to pass up. Over the years Mr. Kimball had developed a correspondence with the Rebbe, and at that pivotal moment he decided to write to the Rebbe for advice. As it happened, he had another piece of news to share: his wife was expecting a baby.

The Rebbe gave his blessings for the upcoming birth, and then addressed the bank's request. "It is clear that the general conditions which affect the problem… are of a nature which change from time to time. Indeed, as you write, this is also the reason that caused the problem of financing. At any rate, it seems at this moment that the next step does not depend on you…" Since Mr. Kimball did not want to sign personally for the loan, it seemed things were out of his control.

The Rebbe continued that while Mr. Kimball could not change the bank's mind, he could gain clarity by strengthening himself spiritually: "While it may appear mystical, it has been borne out by experience and proved quite practical. When a Jew strengthens his bond with the Source of wisdom, which is G-d, he gains wisdom and understanding also in mundane affairs, which helps him to decide what to do and what not to do in matters of business and the like."

The Rebbe then made a reference to Mr. Kimball's profession. "In a legal suit, the best and weightiest argument is when one can cite a precedent from a similar case, and there is no need to substantiate and explain the reason for the judgment further, since the judgment speaks for itself."

The Rebbe wrote that from "precedent," his experience with others, increasing one's commitment to Torah and mitzvahs brings positive results.

In the post-postscript of the letter, the Rebbe made a point he had made to many others: risky business was not worthwhile. "Regarding the project in Nicaragua in general," the Rebbe wrote, "in light of the economic and political situation [there], it does not appear to be a practicable and

Mr. Kimball (right) and the Rebbe.

realistic project in the near future."

The Rebbe was referring to renewed efforts by local priests and outside human-rights groups to condemn the human rights violations of the Somoza government. Earlier that month, guerrillas affiliated with the opposition group in the country had raided a party in the house of the minister of agriculture and taken hostages, among them several leading Nicaraguan officials and Somoza relatives. To many this might have seemed merely a bump in the road, but the Rebbe assessed the risk differently. The government might be stable now, but who knew what the future would bring?

Mr. Kimball took the Rebbe's advice and resisted pressure to sign for the loan. Over the next five years Nicaragua descended into turmoil, and when the Somoza regime ended in 1979, the country defaulted on its debts.

Mr. Jeffrey Kimball.

JUST LIKE YOUR GRANDFATHER

Rabbi Meir Halberstam led a branch of the Sanz Hasidic dynasty, and was known as the Tshokover Rebbe of Bnei Brak. He was once in a private audience with the Rebbe, where he expressed his distress that his son was working in a restaurant, which he felt was not befitting for a descendant of such a respected branch of Hasidism.

The Rebbe responded, "Wasn't our grandfather also a restaurateur?"

Rabbi Halberstam did not understand the Rebbe's statement, and could not think of anyone in his family who owned a restaurant.

The Rebbe explained, "Didn't our forefather Abraham prepare and serve food to whoever entered his tent?"

"But didn't Abraham provide this service for free?" asked the Hasidic leader.

The Rebbe answered, "That was the case only if they agreed to say the Grace after Meals. But if the guest chose not to, he had to pay."

LAWYER III

To become a lawyer takes years of study. To become an expert in a specific field of law takes many more. In order to proceed with a case, the client acquires some basic knowledge of the laws, but will always defer to the lawyer's expertise.

Lay people should be knowledgeable in Jewish philosophy and law. But for a final ruling, one defers to an expert.

LOCKSMITH

Most homes have locks on their doors. The owners choose when to lock the door and when to leave it unlocked.

We too have "doors" through which we take in the information and ideas that form our attitude and view of the world. Like physical homeowners, we need to install "locks," discriminating between ideas we should absorb and those we should not.

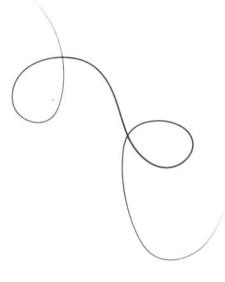

LOCKSMITH II

When you have the key to a house, you have access to everything inside.

At times it is challenging to help others. It is difficult to visit the sick; it could be hard to give an interest-free loan or to find a job for someone out of work. The key is to love your fellow as yourself. Then every good deed becomes accessible.

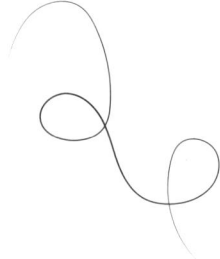

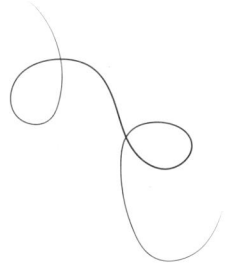

MANICURIST

You might let your nails grow when you're alone, but if you were attending a business meeting or expecting guests, you would trim them.

In the inner sanctum of your heart, confront your own shortcomings, feel the pain they cause, and resolve to overcome them. But with others, "trim your nails"—focus on the good and speak in a positive tone.

DON'T DENY THEM A LIVELIHOOD!

It was March 1972, and thousands of people from around the world had arrived at Lubavitch world headquarters for a grand Hasidic gathering, or farbrengen. The Rebbe was turning 70, but he was not slowing down.

"Age makes my life more exacting," the Rebbe told a New York Times reporter. "My age is demanding more of me."

At the gathering, the Rebbe refused personal presents, but requested a much larger commitment from his Hasidim and himself: 71 new Chabad institutions.

"I think that is a very good challenge, not only for me. It is a very good challenge for them," the Rebbe told the reporter.

Standing in the packed synagogue, London diamond dealer Bobby Vogel felt he had to participate in the new initiative, but how?

Mr. Vogel had recently established a diamond-setting school. It began when an acquaintance got in trouble with the law and could not find employment. The diamond dealer taught the man how to set diamonds. When he had mastered the trade, Mr. Vogel decided to employ him to teach others.

At his manufacturing center in the London diamond district of Hatton Garden, Mr. Vogel dedicated an entire floor to the trade school. Many from the Hasidic community applied. There was a nominal fee, but the diamond dealer rarely collected it, and actually provided a weekly stipend for those who had no other employment.

Many in the diamond district viewed the school with skepticism. Not only was Mr. Vogel wasting money, they said, he was creating competition for himself.

A gathering in honor of the Rebbe's birthday, circa 1980.

In addition to the operating expenses of the school, there was the cost of the diamonds that the students practiced on. Often they were chipped or broken in the process, and became unusable. For Mr. Vogel, however, the satisfaction of providing a livelihood for others made it all worthwhile. "What will I take to the next world?" he would ask. "The broken diamonds from the trade school."

That day in 1972, Mr. Vogel decided that the school would be his birthday present to the Rebbe—one of the 71 new Chabad institutions.

In a private audience, he told the Rebbe of his intention, and suggested naming it "Lubavitch Trade School."

"G-d forbid!" the Rebbe said.

Mr. Vogel was taken aback. Was the Rebbe rejecting his gift?

"It could be that a Hasid of another community would want to learn a trade," the Rebbe told Mr. Vogel. "And because it is called 'Lubavitch,' he won't join the setting school. How can you withhold a Jewish person's livelihood?"

MARKETER

Companies spend millions of dollars on marketing to convince the public to purchase their products. One popular advertising tactic is to feature testimonials from happy customers.

You can be G-d's marketer. When you do a good deed, don't be afraid to tell others about it. Perhaps they will be inspired to follow your example.

MECHANIC

When a car is overused, it burns out more quickly. When it is underused, the battery will not be able to retain its energy, the engine may rust, and other issues can arise.

While you should not overburden your body, not being active can make you sluggish and rusty. A healthy balance is the best way.

MECHANIC II

A car's engine starts with a spark from the starter. If an engine constantly needs to be restarted, it has to be repaired so that it can keep itself running.

Though most of our divine service we need to be self-motivated, at times G-d sends us a "spark" of inspiration. When we use these sparks well, they will keep us going for a long time. If the sparks are very frequent, however, it may be a sign that we need a spiritual tune-up.

WHAT IS RETIREMENT?

Chana Sharfstein was surprised when the Rebbe inquired about her uncle during a private audience. Rabbi Nathan Zuber of Roselle, New Jersey, served as rabbi of the Beth David Synagogue for many decades.

"He has just retired and is doing well," she responded.

The Rebbe shook his head. "Retired—what does that mean?"

Mrs. Sharfstein began to explain that as its members aged, her uncle's congregation had dwindled in size. The synagogue would be closing its doors.

"There is no such thing as retiring," the Rebbe said. "Situations may arise... that necessitate change, and one must then make the appropriate adjustments. But retirement—never!"

The Rebbe then suggested various options for the rabbi, including moving to New York City, where he could involve himself in scholarly pursuits. The Rebbe emphasized that he should continue to use his talents and capabilities to contribute to the Jewish world.

The Rebbe gives Chana Sharfstein a dollar for charity and a blessing.

MERCHANT

When a merchant knows that by waiting a week to sell his goods he will make double the profit he would make today, he will surely choose to wait.

You may feel that the good deeds you have done deserve an immediate reward from G-d. But know that in G-d's goodness, He will pay you back when He understands it will be most "profitable" for you.

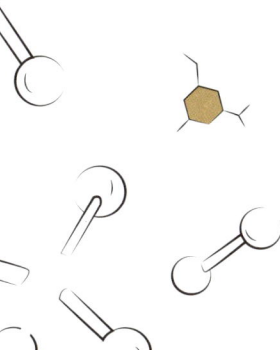

MICROBIOLOGIST

An antibiotic taken many times will eventually lose its effectiveness. The bacteria become resistant, and the doctor changes the medication or increases the dose to heal the patient.

When you are used to a certain dose of prayer, Torah study and mitzvahs, you may stop feeling the positive effects on your daily life. If this happens, increase the amount of time and effort you invest in your observance, and it will once again invigorate your day.

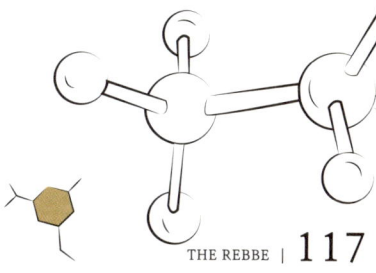

MORTGAGE BROKER

If you purchase a home with a mortgage, until you repay the loan, you do not fully own it.

Our bodies and souls are on loan from G-d. As our sages teach, we were "created to serve [our] Creator" (Talmud, Kiddushin 82a). We cannot consider the debt repaid until we have completed our mission in this world.

HOW TO SPEAK TO AN EMPLOYEE

Born and raised in Jerusalem, Binyomin Klein arrived in Brooklyn to study at the Central Lubavitcher Yeshivah in 1956. In his free time, he assisted the chief aide to the Rebbe, Rabbi Chaim Hodakov, with various duties.

Upon completing his studies, Rabbi Klein married Laya Schusterman, and the couple moved to Melbourne, Australia, to assist with Chabad activities in that country. When the Kleins returned to the United States in 1964, Rabbi Hodakov invited Rabbi Klein to become one of the Rebbe's aides, and he quickly agreed.

Rabbi Hodakov then told him, "I cannot tell you not to hear anything, because there is no way you won't hear what is going on. I cannot tell you not to see anything, because there is no way you will not see what is happening. However, one word of caution: do not talk. Do not repeat to others what you have heard or seen here in these offices."

The Rebbe had a demanding schedule and work ethic, which also became demanding on his aides. Yet, during the many years that Rabbi Klein worked as the Rebbe's aide, when the Rebbe called him to his office, he would say, "If it is not too hard for you, please do the following..."

And when Rabbi Klein completed a task, the Rebbe never failed to thank him.

The Rebbe never failed to thank Rabbi Klein (right).

MOUNTAIN CLIMBER

Scaling a steep mountain, climbers either go up or down. They may stop to rest, but they cannot remain stationary for long.

We constantly need to ascend in our divine service. If we lose our upward momentum, gravity will quickly take over.

MOUNTAIN CLIMBER II

Climbing a mountain requires much more strength and exertion than coming back down. But the sense of accomplishment the climb brings is much greater too.

It is easy to focus on the negative. Actively searching for the good in those around you and seeking ways to make the world better is harder than climbing a mountain. However, it is this approach that will ultimately keep your service of G-d alive and vibrant.

MUSICIAN

Music can express deep emotions and inner feelings more articulately than words.

In the melody of life, each action should be imbued with purpose and emotion. When our actions are meaningful and performed with the correct spiritual intentions, they will perfectly express our innermost being. This can be achieved by studying the teachings of Hasidism.

KEEPING BUSINESS FRESH

Famed tenor Jan Peerce didn't want to retire. Considered to have the longest career of any tenor, Mr. Peerce sang into his late 70s. "At an age when most tenors have been long retired, Mr. Peerce kept on singing, his voice in a remarkable state of preservation," the New York Times once wrote.

Mr. Peerce was a perfectionist. He was proud that he was able to record without using the new techniques for editing and enhancement. "What you hear on the record is what we did right after leaving the control room: no splicing, no *schmeissing*, no fixing, no dropping in of just one note," he wrote in his 1976 autobiography. "When you hear such a recording, you're not hearing real singing; you're hearing a feat of engineering."

But the "modern sound" had become popular, and Mr. Peerce felt squeezed. In a private audience, at which he presented the Rebbe with many of his recordings as a birthday gift, Mr. Peerce told the Rebbe that the market wasn't interested in his albums and that he planned to stop making them.

In a subsequent letter, the Rebbe thanked him for the gift. "Needless to say, I could not resist the urge to hear [them] at least in part, despite the crowded schedule of activities," the Rebbe wrote.

The Rebbe wrote that Mr. Peerce did not require his recommendation, for his G-d-given gift was widely acclaimed. However, "a record, as the name implies, is not only for the present, but also for the long term."

It was important that the singer continue to record, if only for his own personal gratification, the Rebbe added. New recordings would also increase interest in his performances and public appearances,

Mr. Jan Peerce in concert, circa 1976.

which he planned to continue. The Rebbe encouraged Mr. Peerce to make many more records.

The United States public has many great qualities, one being its involvement in charity, but it also has its peculiarities, the Rebbe wrote. "One of them—the tempo of American life. Considering the rapid pace of American life, it is good to be able to refer to a recently published record, rather than one that appeared a long time [ago]."

Mr. Peerce took the Rebbe's advice and continued to record until he was physically unable to.

"He made films, he taught," the New York Times obituary reported, "he recorded, he appeared on television talk shows, and remained one of the busiest singers before the public."

NURSE

In a hospital, the doctor sees the patient briefly to diagnose the illness and prescribe treatment. The nurses spend more time with the patient, making the treatment tolerable with their tenderness and patience.

G-d has given us a prescription for life, and it is our responsibility to share it with others. However, it needs to be done with compassion, sensitivity and patience.

OPTOMETRIST

We depend on our eyes to navigate a path through the physical world.

In the same way, we use our understanding to "see" the possible consequences of each decision we make and to choose the right path.

OPTOMETRIST II

Each eye sees from a different angle, and the brain combines the two views into a single image.

On a spiritual level, the right eye sees only the good in others, while the left eye looks with judgment, noticing the negative. Our job is to create a harmonious outlook in which kindness prevails over judgment.

OPTOMETRIST III

When one sense is blocked, the others automatically become heightened. Thus a blind person's sense of hearing is often much more sensitive than a sighted person's.

G-d created the world so that all we see is the natural order—the universe seems to function on its own. This illusion makes it more difficult for us to hear and understand the truth—that G-d runs the world, down to the smallest detail. However, if you sensitize yourself properly, you will recognize the hand of G-d in your daily life.

PHARMACIST

Pharmacies stock many different kinds of medications to cure a variety of ailments. Yet when you are sick it is not enough to just walk into the pharmacy. First a doctor prescribes a medication, then you bring the prescription to be filled at the pharmacy, and finally you take the medication as the doctor instructed.

Your job is to cure the illnesses of this world with the medicine of Torah. In order to do this, you need a mentor or leader who can prescribe the course that you should follow, and of course you have to follow the instructions.

A MODEL BUSINESSMAN

The Sheftel family was a mainstay of the Jewish community in Worcester, Massachusetts, helping to found the city's Chabad school. In the 1930s, Milton Sheftel married Sophia Ulman, the daughter of fervent Hasidic Jews. Like many others in their generation, they thought that a religious lifestyle would prevent them from achieving professional success, and thus abandoned their Jewish observance.

The Sheftels had a son, Larry, and at the encouragement of the Ulman grandparents, they briefly enrolled him in the Chabad school in Worcester. During the short period when Larry attended the school, the family opened Reed Plastics Corporation. The business was successful, and the newly wealthy Sheftels slowly returned to their Jewish roots, becoming heavily involved in the local Reform temple.

In the 1960s, Larry and his wife found themselves craving a more traditional prayer experience, and began attending the Chabad synagogue in Worcester. Eventually they decided to send their children to the Chabad school Larry had briefly attended as a child.

The small Jewish community in Worcester followed the younger Sheftel couple's journey with interest. Larry, now the president of the plastics company, seemed to be living proof that Jewish observance need not interfere with success in business.

In 1988, the Sheftels sold Reed Plastics to Sandoz Chemical Corporation for a large sum. Larry continued to work as the director of development at Dicer Corporation in Haverhill for some time after the sale, but soon began to feel that he needed a break from business.

The Sheftels always lived modestly, despite their wealth. "Money is not important in life. Everyone needs money, but it is a just facilitator," Larry likes to say. "The most important thing you need is a solid grounding of faith and morality."

At a private audience in September 1991, Larry told the Rebbe, "I have enough money to live comfortably, to give charity comfortably, and to do everything comfortably. I'm thinking to learn Torah for two hours a day, and to help Chabad for two hours a day." He wanted to assist his local Chabad rabbi, Rabbi Herschel Fogelman, with fundraising.

The Rebbe raised two objections to this plan: Larry was then in his early fifties, and the Rebbe felt he could use his time more productively. Second, the Rebbe emphasized that by continuing to work in the business world, Larry would be "sanctifying G-d's name," creating a positive impression on people who otherwise might not encounter a proud Jew.

The Rebbe acknowledged that it was strange for him to be advising someone to pursue business rather than study Torah. "Nevertheless, it is a good idea to show an example of a successful businessman who has set times every day to learn Torah," he said.

Larry took the Rebbe's advice, and continued working in the plastics and real estate fields for many years.

PHARMACIST II

Pharmacies stock strong drugs that could be dangerous for a healthy person. In the correct dosage, however, these medications can heal people who are gravely ill.

When we teach people about Judaism, it needs to be in a positive, loving way. When someone is spiritually ill, however, it may be appropriate to use strong medicine by making it clear that some actions will have a negative effect.

PHYSICIAN

If a patient refuses part of the treatment a doctor prescribes, the doctor will continue with the partial treatment in the hope that the patient will eventually come to his or her senses and follow through with the rest.

When first introduced to Torah, G-d's prescription for life, people may not be ready to accept the entire "treatment." They should nevertheless begin with whatever part they can accept. Eventually, they will follow through with the rest.

PHYSICIAN II

When one limb of the body is weak, the doctor will care for that part, but will also work on strengthening the other, healthy limbs. Building up the body as a whole has an immediate positive effect on its weaker parts.

The Jewish nation is one body. If we see that another person has a spiritual weakness, one way to help is to build up our own spiritual strength.

PHYSICIAN III

A malfunction in the body can be corrected with various therapies. A cancerous growth, however, cannot be corrected. The growth needs to be removed and then the area treated with radiation to ensure that no malignant cells remain.

When people are calculated in their actions, mistakes can be addressed—malfunctions can be corrected. But in this generation, young people have a tendency to act out of chutzpah, simply because they want to. To overcome this challenge, we should employ the teachings of Hasidism, which explain a person's place in the world, why every action has global ramifications, and the humbling nature of G-d's benevolence to us.

PHYSICIAN IV

One of a pediatrician's responsibilities is to vaccinate young children against disease. When a child is later exposed to the disease, he or she will not catch it, or will have only mild symptoms.

A strong Jewish education will inoculate our children against the negative influences in the world, and make the challenges they do face easier to overcome.

A LESSON FOR THE PHLEBOTOMIST

It made international headlines when the Rebbe suffered a heart attack during the holiday of Simchat Torah in 1977.

"The 75-year-old leader of the world Lubavitch movement was participating in the services in the Lubavitch synagogue when he turned pale, complained of feeling tired and sat down," the *Jewish Telegraphic Agency* reported. "The usual Simchat Torah celebration, attended by thousands of Lubavitch members and visiting Jews, was cancelled yesterday."

Doctors predicted that the Rebbe would not return to complete health. "The Rebbe's blood pressure dropped," Dr. Ira Weiss would later recall. "The Rebbe operated at such a high energy output… we could not expect him to function at such a level anymore."

But the Rebbe had no intention of slowing down. Two nights after the heart attack he delivered a 21-minute radio address from his study, though his doctors had asked that he limit it to a few minutes.

The cardiologists who converged on Lubavitch world headquarters to care for the Rebbe marveled at his stamina and wisdom. At one point, a routine medical procedure evoked a deep insight:

"What causes the blood to be drawn?" the Rebbe asked. "Is it the needle, or the void in the syringe?"

The doctors explained that the void in the syringe draws the blood out.

"I once told someone who told me he felt empty," the Rebbe related, "that something void has the power to draw holiness in much quicker. Therefore he is a much more suitable vessel for good."

The Rebbe asked that this exchange be related to those gathered in the synagogue below.

The Rebbe's cardiologist Dr. Ira Weiss.

PILOT

Today, a journey that would have taken months at the turn of the 20th century can be accomplished in a few hours. A message that might have taken weeks in the mail can be delivered instantly over the phone.

The same should apply to our spiritual endeavors. Spiritual growth and good deeds should be accomplished swiftly, breaking through limitations of time and place.

PILOT II

Cruising at 30,000 feet, looking out at the clear blue sky, it's hard to imagine that you are traveling hundreds of miles per hour. Only when you descend to a lower altitude and see houses, trees and roads rushing past do you grasp how fast the airplane is moving.

It's easy to become complacent when it seems that nothing is changing in the world around you. If you look closely, however, you will see that people are constantly moving and growing. This should inspire you to change and grow yourself.

PILOT III

The engines on an airplane create powerful jets that propel the plane forward and upward in the opposite direction.

Our bodies crave physical pleasure; our natural tendency is to be self-centered and animalistic. Not only can we overcome these desires and tendencies, we can use them as opposing "jets" to propel us into higher, more altruistic lives.

PRESIDENT

If the president were to give you a precious instrument, surely you would use it for its intended purpose with reverence.

G-d gave you intellect. He wants you to use it properly and not waste it. The only question is, what will you do with it?

PRISON WARDEN

Ideally, prison should provide criminals with an opportunity to contemplate their wrongdoing and resolve to do better in the future.

The soul descended from the spiritual world, where it basked in divine light, into a physical body, a materialistic "prison." But this descent is only for the purpose of an even greater ascent. For when the soul uses the body to accomplish spiritual aims, the "prison" itself is elevated in holiness.

LECTURE WITH A SECRET AGENDA

Professor Velvl Greene was a microbiologist working for NASA when he began a lengthy correspondence with the Rebbe in the early 1960s. They developed a close relationship, and Professor Greene employed his knowledge and professional credentials at the Rebbe's behest on many occasions.

A serious scholar, Professor Greene delved into Jewish textual study. Eventually he would lecture around the world, telling audiences unapologetically that science and Judaism are completely compatible.

In 1982, General Secretary Leonid Brezhnev was continuing to expand the Soviet army, and analysts were predicting that the Cold War would continue indefinitely. Chief among the Communists' goals was the obliteration of Jewish life, particularly among the youth. Under the Rebbe's guidance, however, a clandestine Chabad network offered Jews of all ages the opportunity to practice Judaism in secret.

Word reached the Rebbe that three professors had joined secret Torah classes taught by Chabad rabbis, and that they had questions about contradictions between Judaism and science. The Rebbe had an aide contact Professor Greene and ask if the professor could arrange an invitation to be a visiting lecturer in the Soviet Union. "The Rebbe wants you to travel to Russia to speak to them," the aide told him, referring to the professors.

The details were arranged with the Soviets, Chabad headquarters sponsored the trip, and Chabad rabbis in London packed Professor Greene's bags with Jewish ritual items, Jewish books and kosher food.

Once there, the professor spent several days with the scientists discussing and resolving their questions.

A clandestine Torah class organized by the Chabad underground in the Soviet Union.

RANCHER

The animals on the farm do not lift their heads up to look at the sky. Only humans raise their eyes and contemplate the heavens.

You could choose to look down and be depressed about your situation, or you could look upward and understand that everything happens by divine providence.

SAILOR

In a boat, we can harness the ocean's power to travel great distances. But the ocean can be a dangerous place, and most boats are equipped with a variety of safety mechanisms and extra precautions, such as life vests and lifeboats.

When our souls descend into the "dangerous waters" of the physical world, G-d provides a vessel, a way of life that allows us to travel safely above the waves and prevents us from drowning in our materialistic existence. We need only enter the ship and follow the safety instructions.

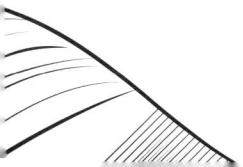

SAILOR II

While the mechanic works below the deck to maintain the engine, it is the captain and sailors who set the ship's course and make sure that it arrives at its destination.

G-d granted you free will to fulfill your mission in this world. If you perform your job well, you, like the mechanic, contribute to the larger vessel's smooth functioning. But do not forget that it is ultimately G-d who steers the ship.

SECRETARY

A secretary reminds those in the office about upcoming obligations.

We need to constantly remind ourselves that we are in this material world for a higher purpose: to serve G-d and reveal His presence here.

NOT JUST A BUSINESS TRIP

Diamond dealer Bobby Vogel was radiant with the love of life. The owner of N. Vogel and Company would travel regularly to Sweden, Switzerland and Gibraltar, and the Rebbe would invariably encourage him to spread Judaism wherever he went.

Before one of his trips to Sweden, the Rebbe gave him one hundred dollars, telling him to purchase mezuzahs for the Jewish community there. "Make sure that you meet all the members of the Jewish community," the Rebbe said.

On another occasion in the early 1970s, the Rebbe told Mr. Vogel to give his best wishes to the president of the congregation in Gibraltar. The territory has a small Jewish community.

"I would like to have a Jewish library in Gibraltar," the Rebbe said, and asked that Mr. Vogel bring it up when he met the president. "A special room should be dedicated for the library, and you should donate the first Jewish books."

It turned out that the Rebbe had more than books in mind: "It could be that a Jewish girl and boy will want to read various books," the Rebbe said with a smile. "They will go to the library, meet each other, and the outcome will be another Jewish family."

A room was duly dedicated in the local Jewish day school for a library.

PASSIVE INVESTORS

In March 1991, Bruno Goldberger came to ask the Rebbe's advice about a real estate investment he was considering in Brussels, Belgium. Did the Rebbe think investing in the city was a good idea?

The Rebbe told him to proceed, especially as the city was becoming an international destination.

Mr. Goldberger then asked if he and his partner should recruit other investors to participate.

"Outside investors are good," the Rebbe said. "However, they should be passive investors," meaning that they would not have a say in the day-to-day management of the investment.

If you give them a say, they will always be interfering without knowing all the details, the Rebbe explained.

"Work with your own money, but if they [want to] give a small amount... it is something that assists," the Rebbe said.

SECURITY GUARD

The more expensive a home or the more precious a store's merchandise, the more security is required.

The more Torah you study, the more spiritual and refined you grow, the more devious the evil inclination will become. Guard yourself carefully.

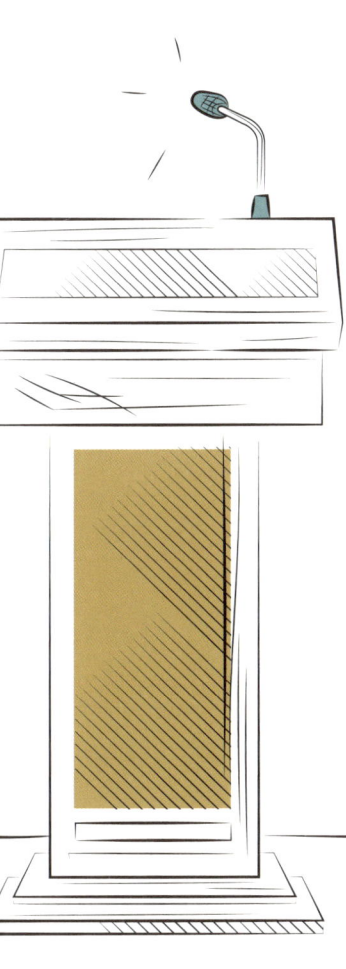

SENATOR

After the debates and discussions on the senate floor, the striking of the gavel signals that a resolution or bill has passed.

We cannot forgo any good deed or mitzvah, for who knows when the final gavel will strike and the proceedings of this life will be completed?

SHIP CAPTAIN

A captain does not abandon ship. If a vessel is truly doomed, the captain will first ensure that everyone on board has been rescued, and only then will he or she leave.

The duty of the "captains" of a Jewish community is to remain where they reside. First and foremost it is their obligation to ensure that everyone else has what they need.

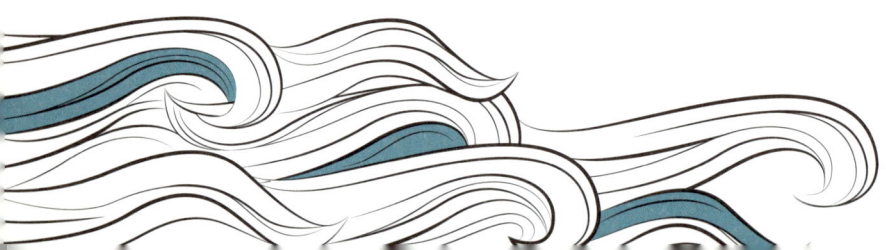

ANOTHER'S LIVELIHOOD

Hundreds of letters from across the globe were delivered to the Rebbe daily. Some asked advice about health issues or financial troubles, engaged couples discussed their upcoming weddings, Torah scholars presented difficult questions in Jewish law and philosophy, and Chabad representatives around the world asked for blessings and guidance.

In 1966, in the midst of the High Holidays, a heart-wrenching letter arrived on the Rebbe's desk. A man in Israel was about to lose his job, for reasons the letter did not divulge. The man's family had written to his Swedish employer, describing the devastating effect the loss would have on the extended family the man supported. But they had not received a response.

As a last resort, the man's brother wrote to the Rebbe and asked him to intervene with the employer. Neither he nor his brother had ever met or corresponded with the Rebbe. The family hoped that the Swedish Jew would take a request from the Rebbe seriously.

With great pain, the man's brother pleaded with the Rebbe to help. "Have mercy on us," he wrote. "If he loses his job, he will not have food to place on his table, please do something about the situation."

The Rebbe had no connection with the Swedish businessman. Yet, contrary to his long-standing custom to not give advice unless someone approached him, the Rebbe wrote to him.

"This request may be seen as meddling into your private issues," the Rebbe wrote. "However, since this has to do with the good of a fellow Jew, I am going out of my normal boundaries, with the hope that you will judge me favorably and grant my request."

The Rebbe enters a Hasidic gathering at Lubavitch world headquarters.

The Rebbe wrote that as a Jew to a Jew, "although we never met face to face, surely you will do all that you can to keep the man... in his employment that gives him his [only] livelihood."

The Rebbe promised that in the merit of sustaining another family, G-d would surely bless him in abundance.

"Please forgive me for meddling into your business matters without your asking," the Rebbe concluded. "With honor and blessings to be sealed to have a sweet new year."

SHOEMAKER

A shoe protects the foot from dirt, bumps and sharp items on the road.

The road of life contains much dirt, many bumps and a variety of "sharp items." The mitzvahs protect us from these spiritual dangers.

SHOEMAKER II

To obtain leather to make shoes, the tanner uses a multistep process that includes tanning, liming and bleaching. The harsh chemicals and machines transform a rough hide into smooth, supple leather.

We are born with a "thick hide," an animalistic tendency that urges us to pursue our own self-interest. Before prayers each morning, we can refine our thick skin by studying the teachings of Hasidism that emphasize the coarse nature of the animal soul when compared with the pure G-dly soul. Over time, with intense effort, we may transform the rough hide into pliable leather.

SLAUGHTERER

The ritual slaughterer does not use a chopping or pressing motion. Rather, he draws the sharp blade swiftly across the animal's neck.

Do not repress or chop at the negative habits and evil inclinations that plague you. Rather, pull their passion and fiery desire in another direction—use them in the service of G-d.

LOCATION MATTERS

Fur and skin traders Solomon and Bernard Perrin thought the location of their offices did not make a difference. Their London office in the East End suited them, and they were satisfied with the business there. Then they got a notice from the London City Council that they would have to vacate the premises because a roundabout was going to be built on the corner.

The father and son had several new locations in mind. Most were on London's east side, where the rent was cheaper. As founding members of the London Chabad institutions, they sought the Rebbe's guidance with the move.

The Rebbe was clear: "Get a location in the best part of London." It was a daring idea. The Rebbe wanted them to find an office in the West End, the city's upper-class neighborhood.

The Perrins began searching for the right place. But when they presented the Rebbe with possibilities, he would respond, "Look for a better area."

Eventually they found a place on Bond Street, the prestigious shopping area. The rent was eight times what it would have been in the East End, but the Perrins were now becoming desperate, and they wanted the Rebbe's approval. It arrived. "This is the place," the Rebbe wrote.

The next time the Perrin salesmen traveled to fur companies across England, many agreed to look at the furs for the first time. "They were anxious to purchase goods which came from Bond Street," Mr. Bernard Perrin recalled. "There were no losses. The city council had done us a favor."

The Rebbe in conversation with Mr. Bernard Perrin.

SOLDIER

The army recruitment officer's main concern is physical strength. Is this person strong enough to perform grueling feats of physical endurance? If not, all the good intentions in the world will not help him or her on the battlefield.

In Judaism too the central concern is the physical deed. It is important to have the right intentions, but without action, the war cannot be won.

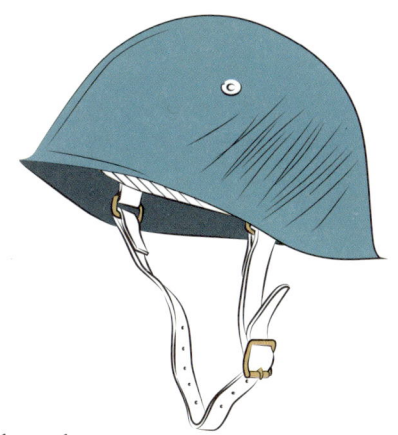

SOLDIER II

In a war, soldiers are most successful when they fight in unity.

When we are unified with our Jewish brethren, the small battles of our everyday lives are more easily won.

SURGEON

A child who walks into an operating theater and sees
a surgeon cutting into an unconscious patient will
naturally assume that something horrible is happening.
As the child grows older, however, he or she will come to
appreciate that the surgeon is actually saving
the patient's life.

It often seems that horrible things are happening,
both in the world at large and in our personal lives. We
may never gain the wisdom to comprehend why these
things happen, but we know that G-d is in charge of this
operation, and He is doing it for our ultimate benefit.

TAILOR

To sew pieces of fabric together, you need a needle and thread. The sharp needle punctures the fabric, making room for the thread that joins the pieces together.

Our mission is to join the physical and spiritual worlds by performing mundane actions for a holy purpose. At times we may need to be as sharp as a needle inside not be ashamed or intimidated. Then we can "sew" the world with mitzvahs and good deeds.

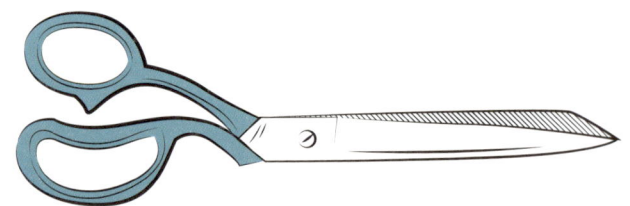

TAXI DRIVER

Without a driver, a car sits idle and useless. In the wrong hands, it becomes a dangerous weapon. But a good driver will use the car safely to travel great distances.

The body is a vehicle for the soul. It is up to us to maintain it and use it for its intended purpose.

INSIDE INFORMATION

By 1967, the Perrin family had been in the fur business for over six decades. Solomon Perrin, the second generation in the business, had been heavily involved in establishing Chabad in London, and that year the community was hoping to build a new Chabad school for girls.

Around this time, Mr. Perrin received an offer to purchase shares in Canadian Devonian Petroleum. He had reliable information that the company would soon be acquired by Shell Oil, at which point he stood to make a fortune. He planned to put all of the profits into the new school building.

Mr. Perrin wrote to the Rebbe, asking for his blessing in the endeavor. "I am willing to mortgage my home to purchase more shares," he wrote.

In his response, the Rebbe suggested that it was not a good investment. After all, there was no guarantee that the deal would go through, and Mr. Perrin obviously had no control over the situation.

The Rebbe added that if Mr. Perrin wanted to learn a lesson, he should purchase £1,000 worth of the shares. The businessman did not understand. How would he be able to finance the school's construction by investing so little?

He followed the Rebbe's advice, however, purchasing a modest number of shares. Over the following weeks and months, he bought the Financial Times daily, scanning the headlines for news of the acquisition. It never happened, and after an oil crisis, the secret deal between the two companies was terminated. Devonian's shares begin to fall, and Mr. Perrin lost most of his money.

The Rebbe enjoys a conversation with an entrepreneur.

TEACHER

The teacher tests the students to see how much they have learned.

Every day G-d gives us tests. If we fail, it's our responsibility to learn the lesson well so that next time we will pass with flying colors.

TELEGRAPH MESSENGER

When people send telegrams, they choose their words carefully, because every letter costs money.

If you knew how precious your every word and action is to G-d, you would be more careful with what you say and do.

TELEMARKETER

A supervisor will often listen in on telemarketers' calls to make sure they are doing a good job.

We cannot forget that our every act, word and thought is being monitored by the Master of the world.

TRAIN CONDUCTOR

There is no point in a locomotive traveling without railcars behind it, and without the locomotive, the railcars have no way to reach their destination. Only together can they achieve their intended functions.

You could neglect your material needs and spend your days immersed in study, or you could reject spiritual pursuits and spend your life chasing physical pleasure. Neither of these approaches will get you anywhere. Only by using spirituality to uplift the physical world can you achieve your purpose.

VINTNER

The wine is hidden in the grape. To enjoy the pleasing taste of the wine, the vintner crushes the grapes.

We may be doing everything we need to in the service of G-d, and yet something is missing. In order to bring out the "wine" that is hidden within us, the ego needs to be crushed. The recognition and contemplation of our own smallness, and of G-d's incredible kindness in choosing us to fulfill His will—this will extract the essence of our souls.

WATCHMAKER

Inside a watch there is a complex mechanism composed of gears, wheels and springs. You may look at the face of the watch throughout the day without ever contemplating the apparatus that lies behind it.

When you give a coin to charity, or perform any other mitzvah, a complex spiritual mechanism, designed and implemented by G-d, is triggered. Performing many small actions throughout the day, you never know the springs and wheels that are stirring in your soul.

THE PROFESSOR'S JOURNAL

One of the first conversations NASA scientist Velvl Greene had with the Rebbe was about individual divine providence. The Rebbe told Dr. Greene that everything that happens is for a reason, and that everything one sees and hears contains a lesson in the service of G-d.

A natural skeptic, Dr. Greene was perplexed. What about all the mundane or bad situations and people one encounters in life? What could they possibly have to teach?

The Rebbe related the following story by way of explanation: Rabbi Israel Baal Shem Tov, the founder of Hasidism, was once walking with his students when some of them brought up this very question. Was it really possible to learn from everything one saw and heard? They had recently seen a group of Christians carving a crucifix onto the ice of a frozen lake. What could this sight possibly teach them about divine service?

Think about water, the Baal Shem Tov responded. Water brings purity, both physical and spiritual. Before a woman conceives, she immerses herself in water. We ritually wash our hands upon arising and before eating bread, and we immerse the body before burial.

Water represents holiness. But frozen water is different. Ice symbolizes an attitude of coldness, of indifference toward what is holy and spiritual. This indifference is the opposite of holiness. Frozen water is a fitting substance out of which to carve a symbol of idolatry.

"Divine providence is true for every person," the Rebbe concluded. "Everyone who walks in every street, everywhere in the world, every day."

Professor Velvl Greene delivers a lecture.

As a prominent scientist, Dr. Greene should find it especially easy to recognize divine providence in his life. "You work in the space program. You are a professor in a medical school. You lecture all over the globe and you meet many interesting people," the Rebbe said.

The Rebbe suggested Dr. Greene keep a journal to record episodes of daily divine providence: "Nothing elaborate, just write down a few things at the end of the day. The little things you have seen or heard.

"If you cannot see for yourself the divine providence," the Rebbe concluded, "bring it here and I will assist you."

AFTERWORD: AN UPLIFTING OUTLOOK

It is difficult for human beings to be happy with what they have. The grass is always greener on the other side of the fence, and nowhere is this saying more apt than in the realm of professional endeavor. Yet, our sages state (Ethics of Our Fathers 4:1), "Who is rich? The one who is happy with his lot."

The Rebbe exemplified this teaching. People brought the Rebbe their troubles, and he showed them the good hidden within the sorrow. In the conviction that a person's profession is the result of divine providence, the Rebbe reminded countless individuals of their duty to use their unique situations to spread light and holiness in the world.

To me, the most powerful expression of this attitude came in the aftermath of the Rebbe's heart attack, on Simchat Torah in 1977. While world Jewry prayed for his wellbeing, the Rebbe saw the situation as an opportunity to reach out.

Two days after a massive heart attack, the Rebbe asked permission from the doctors to give an address from his study. This was the talk he had planned to deliver on the holiday.

While the Rebbe's weekday talks were broadcasted live on the radio and across the world via telephone hookup (and later also via satellite television), on Shabbat and Jewish holidays his audience was limited to the crowd in Lubavitch world headquarters.

The Rebbe began that first address after his heart attack by noting that since the talk had been postponed until after the holiday, more people could now participate, which was an advantage.

On other occasions, the Rebbe looked

The Rebbe during a talk, 1986.

for and highlighted the positive characteristics of each country and society. In the mid-1960s Tziporah Sufrin, a dedicated educator at the Lubavitch Primary School in London, had a private audience with the Rebbe.

"Did you have a chance to visit the local schools in New York?" queried the Rebbe. Mrs. Sufrin said she had. "Did you notice any difference between the operation of the schools here and in England?" the Rebbe asked.

Mrs. Sufrin said that in the United States the students seemed more familiar with their teachers, whereas in England they show more respect.

The Rebbe responded: "There is a monarchy in England. From a monarchy the children learn respect for authority."

Another time the Rebbe observed that American youth are willing to take risks and assume additional responsibilities, while France's history of revolution gave its young people the courage to challenge injustice. And in Israel, the Rebbe said, the children are very independent from a young age.

In the same way, the Rebbe pointed to the unique advantages in every profession. When New York Times religion reporter Irving Spiegel approached him during a gathering, the Rebbe told him, "You can reach more people than I can."

Among the many who benefited from the Rebbe's positive outlook was Rabbi Yitzchok Sufrin, administrator of the London Lubavitch House. Rabbi Sufrin's friends had what seemed to him honorable positions running Chabad centers and organizing adult education and youth programs. Though he was a rabbi in a synagogue and taught adult education classes, he was not satisfied with his day job, which involved sitting in an office and dealing with seemingly petty issues.

During a private audience in the 1960s, he brought up this concern with the Rebbe.

"On the contrary, you have an advantage

Rabbi Lew during a class, circa 1970.

that they don't have," the Rebbe told him. His friends had set days when they taught, and they knew what to expect.

"In an office, people come in," the Rebbe said. "You never know who it is going to be. Therefore you have a special role in touching these lives, bringing Judaism to those you spontaneously encounter in your office daily."

Shmuel Lew
London, UK

CREDITS & SOURCES

Please note that the Rebbe's words have been freely adapted from Hebrew, Yiddish and English sources for clarity and brevity. Any errors are those of the compiler. Many of the sources are unpublished and thus include only a date, or are marked as undated where no date appears on the letter. Stories that were heard directly from the source are not noted below.

It is worth noting that many of the lessons above were directed to people who work in those specific fields.

Page 11 *Keter Shem Tov* (Kehot Publications, 2004), sec. 114. ¶ p. 13 Letter, July 1949 (*Igrot Kodesh*, vol. 3, p. 144). ¶ p. 16 **Accountant** Talk, December 6, 1951 (*Likkutei Sichot*, vol. 24, p. 508). ¶ p. 17 **Archivist** Letter, May 3, 1984. p. 20 **Astronomer** Letter, March 4, 1973 (*Igrot Kodesh*, vol. 28, p. 125). ¶ p. 21 **Astronomer II** Talk, June 23, 1979 (*Sichot Kodesh* vol. 3, p. 8). ¶ p. 22 **Architect** Talk, October 18, 1965 (*Likkutei Sichot*, vol. 10, pp. 8ff). ¶ p. 24 **Artist** Letter, December 7, 1967. ¶ p. 25 **Artist II** Letter, April 1, 1951 (*Igrot Kodesh*, vol. 4, p. 223). ¶ p. 26 **Making Art Affordable** *B'Or Ha'Torah* journal, issues 2 and 4; *Kfar Chabad Magazine*, issue 703. ¶ p. 28 **Artist III** Letter, June 11, 1977 (*Likkutei Sichot*, vol. 23, p. 342). ¶ p. 29 **Astronaut** Talk, December 28, 1968. ¶ p. 30 **Attorney General** Letter, February 11, 1975 (*Igrot Kodesh*, vol. 10, p. 360). ¶ p. 32 **Banker** Talk, March 20, 1962 (*Torat Menachem*, vol. ¶ p. 33, p. 186). ¶ p. 33 **Bookkeeper** Private audience, June 1, 1965 (*Guidance from the Rebbe* [Peter Kalms], p. 13). ¶ p. 34 **Imprisoned by Wealth** *Sichot Kodesh 5736*, vol. 2, pp. 32ff; *Howard Hughes: His Life and Madness* (Norton, 1979); *People* Magazine, Jul 30, 1979, *Howard Hughes' Doctor Gives a Chilling Description of His Strange Patient's Final Hours*. ¶ p. 36 **Broadcaster** Talk, March 2, 1961 (*Torat Menachem*, vol. 30, p. 174). ¶ p. 38 **Broad-**

caster II** Talk, September 24, 1983 (*Torat Menachem 5744*, vol. 1, p. 230). ¶ p. 39 **Bus Driver** Letter, April 27, 1972 (*Igrot Kodesh*, vol. 27, p. 397). ¶ p. 40 **Butcher** Talk, July 8, 1950 (*Torat Menachem*, vol. 1, p. 148). ¶ p. 42 **A Businessman Spreads Light** *Torat Menachem 5743*, vol. 3, pp. 1207ff and pp. 1336ff. ¶ p. 44 **Cardiologist** Letter, undated. ¶ p. 45 **Cardiologist II** Talk, January 2, 1965 (*Torat Menachem*, vol. 45, p. 359, footnote 81). ¶ p. 46 **Chemist** Letter, June 4, 1961 (*Igrot Kodesh*, vol. 20, p. 259). ¶ p. 48 **Coast Guard** Talk, January 13, 1965 (*Torat Menachem*, vol. 40, pp. 159ff). ¶ p. 49 **Computer Programmer** Talk, June 26, 1975 (*Sichot Kodesh 5735*, vol. 2, p. 211). ¶ p. 52 **Construction Worker** Letter, June 1, 1973 (*Letters to My Father* [Landow family, 2005], p. 30) ¶ p. 53 **Construction Worker II** Letter, spring 1974. ¶ p. 54 **Dietician** Letter, June 8, 1955. 55 **Electrician** Talk, March 7, 1960 (*Torat Menachem*, vol. 27, page 397). ¶ p. 56 **Engineer** Talk, April 25, 1954 (*Torat Menachem*, vol. 11, p. 224). ¶ p. 60 **Entrepreneur** Talk, July 16, 1951 (*Torat Menachem*, vol. 3, p. 211). ¶ p. 61 **Entrepreneur II** Talk, August 16, 1952 (*Likkutei Sichot*, vol. 2, p. 629). ¶ p. 62 **Entrepreneur III** Letter, January 10, 1955. ¶ p. 68 **Factory Worker** Letter, June 2, 1959 (*Igrot Kodesh*, vol. 18, p. 391). ¶ p. 69 **Farmer** Letter, March 22, 1965. ¶ p. 70 **Farmer II** Letter, October 31, 1976. ¶ p. 71 **Firefighter** Talk, April 19, 1952 (*Torat Menachem*, vol. 5, p. 174). ¶ p. 72 **Firefighter II** Talk, December 2, 1955 (*Torat Menachem*, vol. 15, p. 317). ¶ p. 76 **Fisherman** Letter, March 24, 1980. ¶ p. 77 **Fisherman II** Talk, January 13, 1985 (*Torat Menachem 5745*, vol. 2, p. 1039. See Talmud, Berachot 61a). ¶ p. 78 **Gardener** Letter, January 14, 1979 (*Return to Roots*, p. 26). ¶ p. 79 **Gardener II** Letter, April 13, 1973. ¶ p. 82 **Home Designer** Letter, undated. ¶ p. 83 **Horseman** Talk, June 10, 1950 (*Torat Menachem*, vol. 1, p. 108). ¶ p. 88 **Internship** Talk, April 25, 1954 (*Torat Menachem*, vol. 11, pp. 218ff). ¶ p. 89 **Insurance Broker** Letter, October 16, 1950 (*Igrot Kodesh*, vol. 4, p. 29). ¶ p. 90 **Jeweler** Private audience, 1960s. ¶ p. 91 **Jeweler II** Talk, July 18, 1987 (*Torat Menachem 5747*, vol. 4, p. 102, footnote 35). ¶ p. 94 **Judge** Talk, August 24, 1957 (*Torat Menachem*, vol. 20, p. 233). ¶ p. 95 **Jumper** Talk, June 23, 1957 (*Torat Menachem*, vol. 20, p. 93). ¶ p. 96 **Jumper II** Talk, April 25, 1954 (*Torat Menachem*, vol. 11, p. 227). ¶ p. 97 **Laundry Person** Letter, June 21, 1951 (*Igrot Kodesh*, vol. 4, p. 335). ¶ p. 98 **Law-**

yer** Talk, April 25, 1954 (*Torat Menachem*, vol. 11, p. 223). ¶ p. 99 **Lawyer II** Letter, February 16, 1977. ¶ p. 104 **Lawyer III** Letter, February 16, 1977. ¶ p. 105 **Locksmith** Letter, October 1962 (*Igrot Kodesh*, vol. 22, p. 333). ¶ p. 106 **Locksmith II** Talk, January 12, 1976 (*Sichot Kodesh 5736*, vol. 1, p. 453). ¶ p. 107 **Manicurist** Talk, December 16, 1967 (*Torat Menachem*, vol. 51, p. 301). ¶ p. 110 **Marketer** Talk, February 27, 1954 (*Torat Menachem*, vol. 11, p. 108). ¶ p. 112 **Mechanic** Private audience, 1970s. ¶ p. 113 **Mechanic II** Letter, November 13, 1952 (*Igrot Kodesh*, vol. 7, p. 46). ¶ p. 116 **Merchant** Letter, June 17, 1956 (*Igrot Kodesh*, vol. 13, p. 249). ¶ p. 117 **Microbiologist** Letter, May 6, 1969 (*Shalom Ubracha* [Be'er Sheva, 2012], p. 102). ¶ p. 118 **Mortgage Broker** Letter, November 17, 1982. ¶ p. 122 **Mountain Climber** Talk, September 29, 1956 (*Torat Menachem*, vol. 18, p. 127). ¶ p. 123 **Mountain Climber II** Talk, June 2, 1960 (*Torat Menachem*, vol. 28, p. 117). ¶ p. 124 **Musician** Letter, November 26, 1968. ¶ p. 128 **Nurse** Audience, June 14, 1953 (*Torat Menachem*, vol. 9, p. 101). ¶ p. 129 **Optometrist** Talk, June 2, 1960 (*Torat Menachem*, vol. 20, p. 50). ¶ p. 130 **Optometrist II** Letter, December 7, 1960 (*Igrot Kodesh*, vol. 20, p. 66); letter, November 23, 1953 (*Igrot Kodesh*, vol. 8, p. 57). ¶ p. 132 **Optometrist III** Talk, March 6, 1958 (*Torat Menachem*, vol. 52, p. 105). ¶ p. 133 **Pharmacist** Letter, January 21, 1949 (*Igrot Kodesh*, vol. 3, p. 146); talk, October 9, 1955 (*Torat Menachem*, vol. 15, p. 107). ¶ p. 136 **Pharmacist II** Letter, January 21, 1949 (*Igrot Kodesh*, vol. 3, p. 146). ¶ p. 137 **Physician** Letter, undated. ¶ p. 138 **Physician II** Letter, September 15, 1974 (*Letters to My Father* [Landow family, 2005], p. 39). ¶ p. 140 **Physician III** Talk, June 26, 1953 (*Torat Menachem*, vol. 6, p. 72). ¶ p. 141 **Physician IV** Letter, April 25, 1955 (*Igrot Kodesh*, vol. 11, p. 58). ¶ p. 142 **A Lesson for the Phlebotomist** *Sichot Kodesh 5738*, vol. 1, p. 593. ¶ p. 144 **Pilot** Letter, November 8, 1973 (*Letters to My Father* [Landow family, 2005], p. 39). ¶ p. 145 **Pilot II** Talk, September 29, 1956 (*Torat Menachem*, vol. 18, p. 127). ¶ p. 146 **Pilot III** Letter, May 21, 1975 (*Igrot Kodesh*, vol. 30, p. 224). ¶ p. 147 **President** Letter, January 5, 1966. ¶ p. 148 **Prison Warden** Letter, August 20, 1974 (*Heichal Menachem*, vol. 3, p. 60). ¶ p. 150 **Lecture with a Secret Agenda** *Professor Greene Shalom Ubracha* (Be'er Sheva, 2012). ¶ p. 152 **Ranch-**

er Talk, June 8, 1954 (*Torat Menachem*, vol. 12, p. 42); talk, June 11, 1951 (*Torat Menachem*, vol. 3, p. 147). ¶ p. 153 **Sailor** Talk, August 15, 1987 (*Torat Menachem 5747*, vol. 4, p. 234). ¶ p. 154 **Sailor II** Talk, June 11, 1951 (*Torah Menachem*, vol. 3, p. 153). ¶ p. 155 **Secretary** Letter, undated (*Kfar Chabad*, issue 883, p. 17). ¶ p. 158 **Security Guard** Talk, December 12, 1957 (*Torat Menachem*, vol. 21, p. 240). ¶ p. 159 **Senator** Talk, December 5, 1987 (*Torat Menachem 5748*, vol. 1, p. 605). ¶ p. 160 **Ship Captain** Letter, October 26, 1969 (*Igrot Kodesh*, vol. 26, p. 231). ¶ p. 162 **Another's Livelihood** *Hitvaadut* booklet, Shabbat Vayelech 5776, p. 26. ¶ p. 164 **Shoemaker** Talk, April 23, 1957 (*Torat Menachem*, vol. 19, p. 320). ¶ p. 165 **Shoemaker II** Talk, April 12, 1955 (*Torat Menachem*, vol. 14, p. 35). ¶ p. 166 **Slaughterer** Letter, September 27, 1960 (*Igrot Kodesh*, vol. 20, p. 6). ¶ p. 170 **Soldier** Talk, November 4, 1950 (*Torat Menachem*, vol. 2, p. 90). ¶ p. 171 **Soldier II** Talk, October 15, 1984 (*Torat Menachem 5745*, vol. 1, p. 295). ¶ p. 172 **Surgeon** Letter, May 23, 1956 (*Igrot Kodesh*, vol. 13, p. 171). ¶ p. 174 **Tailor** Talk, August 21, 1989 (*Torat Menachem 5749*, vol. 4, p. 183ff). ¶ p. 175 **Taxi driver** Letter, October 27, 1952 (*Igrot Kodesh*, vol. 7, p. 23). ¶ p. 178 **Teacher** Letter, June 29, 1966 (*Heichal Menachem*, vol. 3, p. 166). ¶ p. 179 **Telegraph Messenger** Talk, June 2, 1979 (*Sichot Kodesh 5739*, vol. 3, p. 100). ¶ p. 180 **Telemarketer** Talk, June 2, 1979 (*Sichot Kodesh 5739*, vol. 3, p. 100). ¶ p. 181 **Train Conductor** Talk, August 16, 1952 (*Torat Menachem*, vol. 6, p. 146); letter, July 3, 1956 (*Igrot Kodesh*, vol. 13, p. 295). ¶ p. 182 **Vintner** Talk, July 28, 1956 (*Torat Menachem*, vol. 17, pp. 153ff). ¶ p. 183 **Watchmaker** Letter, December 26, 1955 (*Igrot Kodesh*, vol. 12, p. 210).

PHOTOS

Agudas Chasidei Chabad Library, Algemeiner Journal, Meir Alfasi, Marc Asnin, Israel Bardugo, Grayson Dantzic, Donal F. Holway, Kfar Chabad Magazine, Michele Studios/The Kahan family, MyEncounter.com, Shana Sureck, Fridrich Vishinsky/Chai Gallery, Rabbinical College of America and United Lubavitcher Yeshivoth.

Some images were not marked with the photographer's name. We regret any omissions.

ACKNOWLEDGEMENTS

The work for this book was begun last spring, under the tutelage and thanks to the generosity of Rabbi Simcha Zirkind, of blessed memory, longtime Chabad pioneer in Tunisia and Canada. The Advice for Life project was his dream—his last will and testament—and I was honored to work closely with him in fulfilling that dream during the last five years of his accomplished life. Standing beside his fresh grave, I promised Rabbi Zirkind that the Advice for Life series would continue. I miss our almost-daily calls, but I still hear his booming voice on the line, "Dovid, what's cookin'?!" Through his efforts, hundreds of thousands were touched by the Rebbe's teachings. This book will surely stand as a merit for his soul.

This year has proved to be a difficult one. I lost several dear friends. My wife, Chana Raizel, stood by my side through thick and thin, and thanks to her I continued to trek along through the ups and downs. Thank you for enriching my life.

There is nothing like good friends and supporters. I owe a debt of gratitude to the Chabad representatives from around the world who have encouraged me to continue the Advice for Life series, despite all the difficulties.

Chana Sharfstein once again proved to be a reliable source of information, wisdom and encouragement. Marc Asnin has long been a loyal friend, assisting me in many endeavors. Yitzchok Yehudah Holtzman and the entire staff of Kfar Chabad magazine were always there when I had a question or needed a favor. It is the vision of the magazine's editor, Aharon Dov Halperin, a pioneer in spreading the Rebbe's teachings, that make publications like this one possible.

The research was daunting. Rabbi Chaim Shaul Brook, Rabbi Mendel Feller, Rabbi Avraham Jaffe, Rabbi Mendel Fogelman, Louise Hager, Zalman Levine, Rabbi Shmuel Lew, Bernard Perrin, Menachem Slavaticki, Chaim Twersky, Rabbis Chuni and Nechemia Vogel, Rabbi Dovid Weitman and Rabbi Shlomo Yaffe are just some of the people who helped in collecting the stories, facts and contact information I needed. A special thank you to all those who agreed to be interviewed.

Thank you to Yona Avtzon, Marc Asnin, Hilary Gale, Mayer Harlig, Rabbi Moshe Herson, Rabbi Avraham Jaffe, the Kahan Family, Menachem Kirschenbaum, Rabbi Noach Kosofsky, Gershon Laufer, Pinchus Lew, Yossel Mochkin, Rabbi Avrohom Rosenfeld, Ezzi Schaffran, Shimmy Schaffran, Batsheva Shemtov and Menachem Wolff for your assistance with the photos.

My sincere appreciation to those who reviewed the text and shared their comments and critique: Rabbi Mendel Feller, Alex Heppenheimer, Rabbi Avrohom Kievman, Rabbi Aharon Leib Raskin, Chana Sharfstein, Rabbi Moshe Zaklikofsky and Shalom Zirkind.

The pages of this book are graced with the art of Yitzchok Moully. It was easy working with this creative mind. Thank you for sharing your talent.

Special thanks to Rabbi Shmuel Lew, the principal at the Lubavitch Senior Girls' School in London, United Kingdom, for his afterword emphasizing the Rebbe's positive outlook in all matters.

Elana Rudnick and her dedicated team at Design Is Yummy for the fantastic design work. Thank you for being flexible in making this work come to fruition. Working with Nelson Paniagua on the printing of this publication has been a pleasure. You were always willing to accommodate our needs, and we are thankful.

Over the years, various individuals have made their collections of rare journal and newspaper articles available to Lubavitch Archives. These treasures come to use daily, and their generosity is greatly appreciated. During this project I made extensive use of the libraries and work spaces of the Yagdil Torah learning center, Mesivta Chovevei Torah, and Agudas Chasidei Chabad Library. The custodians of these organizations deserve my thanks.

With a deep sense of humility, I thank G-d for granting me the strength to reach this new milestone.

"Praise to G-d, for He is good, for his kindness is everlasting."

Dovid Zaklikowski

ABOUT THE ARTIST

Raised by former hippies, Yitzchok Moully grew up off the beaten path and was exposed to much color. Moully's formal education in Jewish day schools in Australia and later at the Rabbinical College of America did not include art classes, but after dabbling in various forms of art, Moully found expression for his creativity in the silkscreen process.

Moully's art contrasts strong Judaic and Hasidic images with vibrant, bold colors to create a startling combination, which he describes as "Hasidic pop art."

The art reveals that the essence of Hasidic thought is far from black and white. Under the black hat, he likes to say, there is a wealth of vibrant, colorful energy waiting to be released.

His work can be seen at www.MoullyArt.com.

לזכות
דוד בן רחל

לעילוי נשמת
ר' זלמן בן ר' זאב
יפה

לעילוי נשמת
התָ' ר' **ישראל אהרן**
בן **הרב חיים דוב בער**
חייטאן

In loving memory of
Mrs. **Brana Shaina**
of blessed memory
Deitsch

לעילוי נשמת

מרת **בראנא שיינא**

בת ר' **אברהם צבי** הלוי

דייטש

נפטרה י"ג תשרי, ה'תשע"ה

More in the series:

Advice for Life: Education

Advice for Life: Marriage

Advice for Life: From Life to Life

Dignified Differences: A Special Soul

Advice for Life: Daily Life

Hasidic Archives books are available in special discounts for bulk purchases in the United States for corporations, institutions, and other organizations. For more information, please contact us at RebbeAdvice@Gmail.com.